First published in 1981 by
Naturalis Verlags- und Vertriebsgesellschaft mbH
Munich–Mönchengladbach

This edition is adapted from the original German edition
of "DIE SCHÖNE WELT DER PFERDE" by
Arnim Basche, Hans Dossenbach, Werner Gorbracht
and Ulrik Schramm.

Publisher: **Kurt Blüchel**

Project Manager: Joachim F. Hamacher
Art Editor: Claus-J. Grube
Picture Editor: Klaus Griehl
English Text Editor: Chester Fisher
Production: Josef Bütler, Zürich
Typesetting: ABC Fotosatz & Repro GmbH, Munich
Reproduction: Ringier & Co. AG, Zofingen
Binding: Sigloch, Künzelsau

Printed in Switzerland by Ringier AG, Zofingen

Library of Congress Catalog Card No. 82-8527
ISBN: 0-531-09880-X

A WORLD OF HORSES

Anne Charlish

**Consultant Editor:
Sally Gordon**

FRANKLIN WATTS
NATURALIS

Foreword by

Alwin Schockemöhle

Olympic champion at
Montreal (1976) and gold
medallist in the team event
at Rome (1980).

The pages of this superb book lay
before the reader all the magic and
beauty of horses. It is a passionate
declaration of the love of horses.
Horse riding, once a sport for the
élite, is developing more and more
into a popular sport. In most Western
countries the number of leisure-time
riders has greatly increased in recent
years. Horse sports, especially showjumping, have gained huge and loyal
audiences. The early 20th century
prediction that horses would become

Alwin Schockemöhle

redundant and possibly an endangered species has not been fulfilled. For those who wish to go beyond the armchair appreciation of horses – a word of caution. Considerable effort has to be made before one can honestly say, "The greatest happiness on earth is to ride on the back of a horse". For anyone who has not sat in the saddle from his earliest childhood the first attempt to ride a horse can be quite a hard test. Patience and perseverance are the foremost requirements; a love of horses is taken for granted. Anyone fulfilling these conditions will experience a thrill that no rider can forego, there is hardly anything more satisfying than roaming through the countryside on horseback or riding in competition with like-minded persons.

Today use of the horse mainly for leisure and sporting pursuits should not, however, allow one to forget the great contribution the horse has made to man's history. Over the centuries

the horse has had to abandon its freedom for domination by man. It changed from a hunted animal to man's most valuable asset in work, transportation and war. The horse has been central in most great historical events and can be said to have changed the history of mankind. It is the world's most versatile animal. I hope that this book will bring about a new appreciation for the personality and qualities of the horse. The photographs of horses in the wild present a fascinating aspect of the horse. Though horses can be trained and disciplined there still remain in them primitive instincts and desire for freedom. Man has not extinguished the essential spark in the horse despite the long association he has had with it.

Especially interesting is the vast wealth of breeds and types of horse which man has bred for the numerous roles required over the centuries – from the sturdy shire horse to the beautiful and svelte Thoroughbred. It is to be hoped that we will maintain every breed for future generations. Every breed has its own character and part to play.

I am sure that this book will delight and enthrall all horse-lovers, hopefully it will also bring in new converts to the fascinating and beautiful world of the horse.

Alwin Schockemöhle

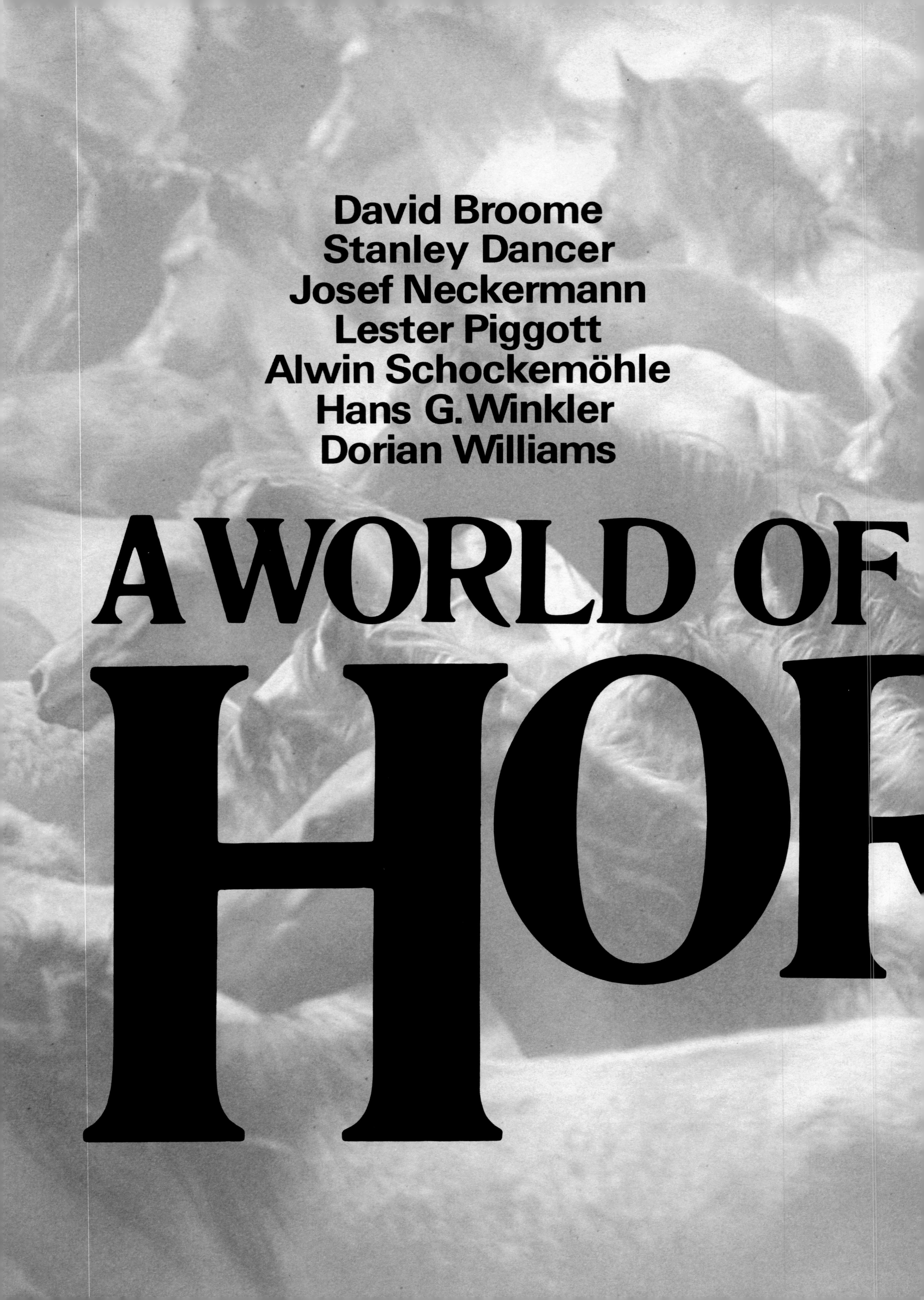

David Broome
Stanley Dancer
Josef Neckermann
Lester Piggott
Alwin Schockemöhle
Hans G. Winkler
Dorian Williams

A WORLD OF
HOR

Anne Charlish

**Consultant Editor:
Sally Gordon**

RSES

Edited by Kurt Blüchel

Contents

Foreword by Alwin Schockemöhle 30

Introduction 38

A 60-Million Year Evolution 60

In the Wild – the Natural Horse 73

The Horse in History – the Great Contribution 132
Introduction by **Dorian Williams** 130

Breeds and Types – A Vast Variety 166
Introduction by **David Broome** 164

Riding Games – Speed and Courage 218

Hunting on Horseback 240

The Spanish Riding School – Riding to Perfection 244

Show-jumping – Spills and Thrills 250
Introduction by **Hans Günter Winkler** 248

Dressage – Precision and Grace 278
Introduction by **Josef Neckermann** 276

Eventing – Speed and Endurance 286

Racing – The Sport of Kings 296
Introduction by **Lester Piggott** 294

Trotting and Pacing – the Modern Charioteers 342
Introduction by **Stanley Dancer** 340

Riding for Leisure and Pleasure 364

Index 382

Introduction

"Where in this wide world can man find nobility without pride, friendship without envy or beauty without vanity? Here, where grace is laced with muscle, and strength by gentleness confined. He serves without servility; he has fought without enmity. There is nothing so powerful, nothing less violent; there is nothing so quick, nothing more patient."

Ronald Duncan

"When I bestride him I soar, I am a hawk. He trots the air; the earth sings when he touches it; the basest horn of his hoof is more musical then the pipe of Hermes."

From Henry V.
William Shakespeare
1600.

"Hast thou given the horse strength? Hast thou clothed his neck with thunder? Canst thou make him afraid as a grasshopper? The glory of his nostrils is terrible. He paweth in the valley, and rejoiceth in his strength: he goeth on to meet the armed man. He mocketh at fear, and is not affrighted; neither turneth he back from the sword."

Book of Job

"Thou shalt be a source of happiness and wealth for man…"

The Prophet
Mohammed

48

"Horse and rider are one being, the will of man and the body of the animal: thus they burst through all deeds and decisions that lie ahead. From this unity grew all nobility and chivalry; grew the tender understanding for the creature which the rough fist can never spur on to great achievements; grew the fearlessness which is transferred from the rider to the horse, and the delight in being able to gallop away into the distance and swiftly overcome the obstacles encountered."

Professor
Richard Gerlach

"When God created the horse, he spoke to the magnificent creature: I have made thee without equal. All the treasures of this earth lie between thy eyes."

Koran

"No other animal has had such an impact on man's attitude as the horse. The first nations of horsemen were regarded as demigods or centaurs by the inhabitants of the Aegean coast, and the American Indians fled as before demons when the first Spanish discoverers rode up to them. The Arabs say that their horses are born 'out of fire and wind', and on horseback they conquered the desert."

Professor
Richard Gerlach

A 60-Million

Year Evolution

There is no species of mammal whose development can be traced back with such impressive clarity as the horse. The research into its evolution has a chain of fossils at its disposal which is more complete than any other, and dates back to the Eocene Age, to that geological era of 35 – 55 million years ago in which the mammals had only just begun to develop properly after the end of the great reptile period.

In 1839 the English paleontologist Sir Richard Owen was given a small tooth which had been found by a tile-maker, together with an almost entire animal skull discovered by an amateur geologist in Kent. Owen named the unknown animal whose remains these were, *Hyracotherium* or "badgerlike animal". Badgers were then considered to be rodents, and Owen described his *Hyracothe-*

rium as "a creature similar to the jack rabbit or some other timid rodent". Owen could not have been expected to know any better at that time. He could not guess then that his *Hyracotherium* was the oldestknown form of horse, because the proportions of the skull as well as of the small, uneven teeth had no similarity at all to the modern horse's skull or teeth. There were no other skeletons known then which would point to a further development of this animal in the form of a horse.

A mere 20 years later Charles Darwin published his *Theory of Evolution*, which shattered world thinking.

Above: Drawings by Stone Age man, such as those in the caves of Altamira and Lascaux, tell us that horses were part of life many thousands of years ago.

Eohippus

Since then, hundreds of researchers have gathered thousands of parts of skeletons, have skeletonized them, measured them and classified them. The most successful of the bone collectors was the American Othniel Charles March (1831–99). From his finds of primitive horse forms from various geological eras he was able to assemble a line of ancestors which contained practically all the more important stages in the evolution of the horse, and which no one has yet been able to extend substantially. March was given for the first time in 1876 the remains of a particularly small primitive form to add to his already numerous collection of fossilized horses, and he named it *Eohippus* and correctly placed it at the beginning of his line of ancestors. Only a few years later March's arch rival Edward Drinker Coppe (1840–97), discovered that *Eohippus* was none other than the *Hyracotherium* previously described by Owen in England. Thus the name *Eohippus* was no longer recognized in scientific terminology. The oldest known primitive horse therefore bears the confusing and tonguetwisting label *Hyracotherium*. However, it continues to be popularly known as *Eohippus* – "Horse of the Ocean".

The ancestors of Eohippus

The line of ancestry of the horse begins for us with *Eohippus*, but of course this strange animal had also in its turn developed from a line of ancestors which originated from a microscopically small one-cell organism many millions of years previously. The full chain is not known but the immediale ancestors of *Eohippus* belonged to a mammal group called the Order of the *Condylarthra*. In the Paleolithic Age, about 50 – 65 million years ago, they were the most important mammals and were to be found in great numbers. Earlier species of these *Condylarthra* stil had the teeth of carnivores, whereas the teeth of the later forms were best suited for chewing up leaves, but they were probably also used to eat small animals. Apart from their preference for plants, there is hardly anything that points to the fact that all known ungulates including horses, cattle deer, pigs, tapirs and rhinoc-

Below: This small bronze horse was probably offered to the gods by primitive man.

eros were to develop from these *Condylarthra*. They were about the size of a cat and they resembled an otter in some respects, with their long-stretched, short-legged form, with the extended, strong tail. As with all primitive mammals, they had five toes on each foot. Most mammals reduced the number of toes in a later stage of their development and so, in this respect, "man is a primitive animal". In the *Condylarthra*, among which it is assumed that the ancestors of the horse were to be found, the middle one of the

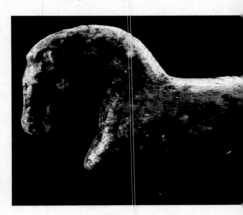

five toes was the biggest and strongest. Even at this point, therefore, a step towards specialization had been made which was to play an enormously important role in the development of the horse.

The descendants of Eohippus

Eohippus, our primitive horse, had o reduced number of toes; it had four on both forefeet and three on the hind feet, and even if it still stood with all these toes on the ground, the preferential evolution of the middle toe could not be ignored. *Mesohippus*, in the Oligocence Age which followed, still had three toes, but only the middle one had a horn cap, which must have already resembled the hoof of a horse. In the case of the *Merychippus* in the Miocene Age, 25–5 million years ago, the side toes had now become small useless attachments, and in the case of the Pliohippus in the Pliocene Age, 5–2 million years ago, the side toes had disappeared. Out of the small animals with several toes which were able to move well on the marshy ground of the ancient landscapes due to the large surface area of its feet, the horse had developed. This was an animal suited to firm, dry ground which, because of the small surface area of the hard hoof, and of course also because of its long legs, was able to reach high speeds, therefore enabling it to escape from its numerous enemies. Less obvious, but just as important, was the development of the horse's teeth. *Eohippus*, similar to the *Condylarthra*, had small, uneven teeth, with which it ate mainly soft leaves and probably also fruits and berries and in addition possibly chewed up small animals. It would not have been able to survive on grass, which at that time was very difficult to find, as it had only just begun to spread across the earth. With the transformation of large areas into steppes, grass became an extremely rich source of nourishment which, however, required specialist eaters. In addition, the open grassland scarcely offered the larger animals protection from being sighted by beasts of prey.

In order to survive here, they had to be powerful, like buffalo, elephants or rhinoceros, or they had to be fast, equipped with keen senses like antelopes or horses. They also had to develop teeth which, with their large, rough, masticating surfaces, would be able to grind the grasses which were rich in cellulose fiber, but teeth which were at the same time able to withstand extreme wear and tear. A man could live on grass for about a year, but by then

his teeth would be worn down completely to the roots. But horses met these requirements superbly in the course of their evolution. By far the largest part of the head of the horse today is taken up by the masticating apparatus in its powerful jaws, in which the teeth sit in deep cavities; the jaws are equipped with very strong masticating muscles. Apart from this and some other alterations to the body structure, horses had to adapt their behavior to suit life in the wide open spaces. They not only had to become fast and tenacious, but they also had to develop a definite nomadic nature, which forced them to cover great distances at particular times of the year so that they could always find sufficient food and drink. They had to develop an instinct in order to be able to flee at the slightest sign of danger without to considering what was happening. As loners, which they probably were at one time, they would have had no chance of survival in the steppes. Only in the community of the herd was there an uninterrupted guard held day and night which gave effective protection against beasts of prey. This, on the other hand, required the development of a social code of behavior. It is this very social behavior that is today one of the most significant psychological characteristics of the horse,

and of great importance to us. It is only thanks to this behavior, which is based on strict hierarchy, that man and horse are able to live together reasonably well. In the next chapter this phenomenon will be studied more carefully.

Many mammals from the Paleocene and Eocene Ages were found in North America as well as in Europe, and this was true also of the *Condylarthra* and *Eohippus*. This is not surprising because in those days North America and Europe were part of a firmly connected continent which was only later split up. But, farther north, between Alaska and Siberia, a small land connection, the so-called Bering Bridge, remained until right into the Ice Age. It was situated in the region of today's Bering Sea. This land bridge is of the utmost importance. Without it there

might be no horses today! Indeed, today we have remains of fossilized horses from every continent except Australia. As a result of its extremely early isolation in the earth's history, horse-like animals were unable to settle there.

The cradle of the horse

On the basis of the fossil finds we have very accurate information about the wanderings and geographical distribution of horses. We know that the cradle for these animals was North America. It is apparent that most of the primitive wild horses had a strong drive to distribute themselves and to settle in large areas. Relatives of at least

This page: **The Stone Age hunter often engraved the walls of his cave dwelling with pictures of the horses and other animals he sought for food.**

1 The oldest known form of the horse lived about 55 million years ago in the Eocene period. It was about the size of a fox with padded feet like a dog's. Hyracotherium, popularly known as Eohippus or the "dawn horse", had three toes on each hind foot and four on each forefoot. Remains have been found in Europe and North America.

2 Mesohippus lived about 40 million years ago in the Oligocene period and was still very small at 20 inches (50 centimeters) high. North America.

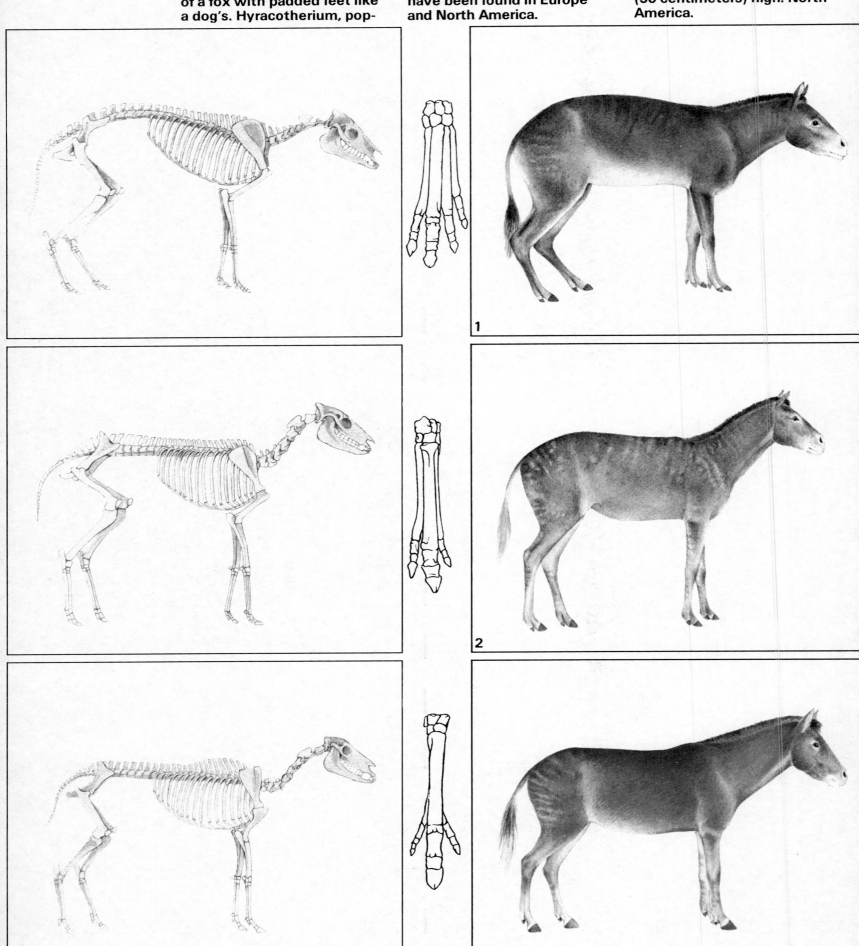

3 Merychippus, the next in the line of evolution of the horse, lived about 25 to 5 million years ago. The two toes at the side have now become vestiges and the teeth have become adapted for grazing the raw fibers of grass, rather than the leaves its ancestors had eaten. North America.

4 Pliohippus was the first type of horse to show a completely undivided hoof with the other toes merely splints. Pliohippus was able to achieve a greater speed with the undivided hoof as he fled the predatory animals that sought him for food. Pliohippus lived about 5 – 2 million years ago and stood about 45 inches (115 centimeters). North America.

5 Plesippus shows a resemblance to today's zebra, which belongs to the same family. It lived in the Pleistocene period.

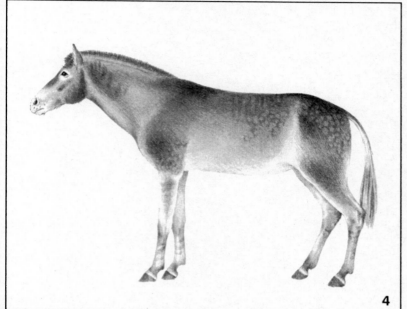

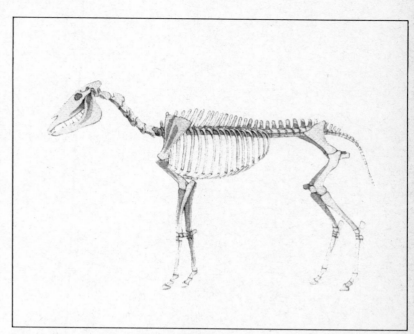

4

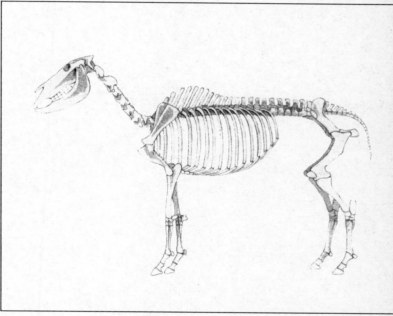

5

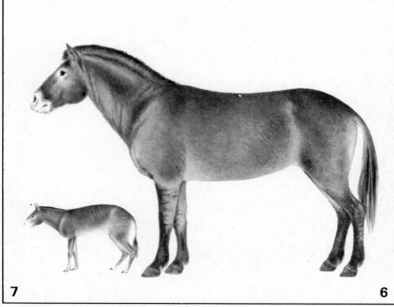

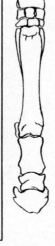

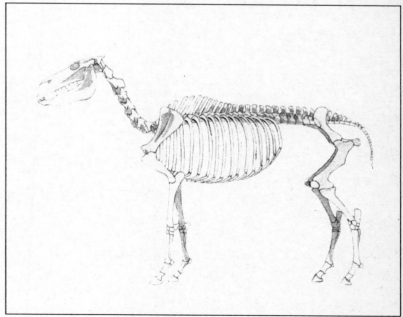

7

6

6 Equus – the first true horse – is the genus to which all hoofed animals (horses, donkeys and zebras) belong. The species shown is Przewalski's horse, which today is the last of the world's wild horses as distinct from those that have escaped domestication to return to the wild.

7 Eohippus was only about one foot (25 centimeters) high; the Przewalski's horse (seen overleaf) some 50 million years later measures about 53 inches (135 centimeters).

65

two early breeds of horses wandered to and fro between North and South America, but they later became extinct in these areas. After the splitting up of North America and Europe members of several breeds succeeded in crossing the Bering Bridge and were able to distribute themselves in Europe, Asia and Africa.

The modern horse
Finally, the most modern breed of horse came into being. It was called *Equus caballus*. The species *Equus* also includes the donkey, ass, onager and zebras. This probably took place in the late Pleistocene Age, about three million years ago. These animals were probably keener on wandering than their ancestors. Several types of the breed created in North America gradually spread themselves across large parts of Asia and Europe down to the very southern tip of Africa.

There are today hundreds of breeds and types of horses all over the world and within those breeds and types an infinite range of color and marking. The origins of the species, *Equus caballus*, is a subject that arouses considerable controversy and disagreement, and a number of theories exist – each of which can be fervently held to be correct. Some people believe that all today's horses have descended from just one type, while others believe that two, three or four types are involved.

While it is possible that all types are descendants of just one, there are

nevertheless four quite distinct basic types to which today's many breeds and types can be traced. These are the the *Forest* type, the *Steppe* horse, the *Plateau* type and the *Tundra* – the latter having had little bearing on today's horses, except possibly the huge horse of the polar regions, the Yakut.

The Forest horse
Together with the Tundra horse, the Forest horse was usually found in fairly cold, wet climates. The Forest horse was a sturdy, solid looking animal with a large head and large feet.

The Steppe horse
The tarpan is the last living reminder of the ancient Steppe horse. Although the last wild tarpan died in the late 1870s, the last captive specimen lived until 1919. The tarpan or rather the tarpan-like horse can still be seen in Poland where a herd that is derived from Polish Konik mares and Przewalski stallions is maintained.

The origins of the tarpan attracts the same degree of controversy that surrounds the past of the horse itself. Some experts maintain that the tarpan may be the European branch of the Mongolian wild horse, the Przewalski, while others believe that both the tarpan and the Mongolian wild horse are separate races of *Equus caballus*, the domestic horse. The Steppe horse is usually regarded as the forerunner of the small, light horse breeds which tend to be of small build with long

limbs. It generally inhabited the warmer climates of Asia and northern Africa.

The Plateau horse
The wild horses of Mongolia, Przewalski's horse, represent the last of the Plateau type which used to roam over Europe and northern Asia. It was only in 1881 that a Russian explorer, Colonel N. M. Przewalski, discovered a small herd of this ancient type surviving in the Gobi desert.

The domestic horse
It would be impossible to trace the evolution of the horse without now acknowledging man's part in its history. Horses originally ran wild, their only contact with man being when they were hunted for food. Perhaps about 5,000 years ago, however, man first started to realize the potential of the horse, and it is from this time that we have many different sorts of evidence on which to base not only the evolution of the horse but man's use. Up until then, research has had to rely on the analysis of fossil deposits, which naturally could impart only the basic form of the horse and the terrain and type of food on which it had existed. Cave paintings from Lascaux in southern France and Altamira Cave in Spain depict the horse as an object of the hunt for food. Stone Age caves have yielded huge piles of horse bones – many of them split open and the marrow extracted.

Above: Tarpan-like horses are found today in Poland: they are the result of crossbreeding between Polish Konik mares **and Przewalski stallions, the most Tarpan-like offspring being retained for breeding.**

This page: **Przewalski's horse was discovered living wild in Mongolia when the Russian explorer, Colonel N.M. Prze-** walski, travelled through the country with a caravan of camels.

India and China

It is not known when man first domesticated the horse but it is thought to be in China and in India. Chinese vases dated to 3,500 BC show the horse being ridden and harnessed, and the Brahmin religion of India has mythological references to Manu, the first human, riding a horse.

It seems probable that man was learning to master the horse from about 3,000 BC in Asia, Europe and North Africa. Pictorial and written records are rare indeed and even archeological finds are scanty. A text from the third dynasty of Ur dating from 2,100 BC, however, describes the horse's flowing tail and implies that it has already been tamed. Sumerian art depicts horses pulling primitive carts and relics from the Persian Gulf show that man used the horse even before 2,500 BC. Modern breeding methods probably only date back two to three hundred years, but the Chinese were among the first to breed speci-

fic types of horses for different purposes some three thousand years ago. Although man was by then in the process of domesticating the horse, thousands and thousands remained wild all over the world – with the notable exception of America, where the horse had become extinct some 7,000 years earlier.

The horse and man

The ancient Egyptians are believed not to have ridden the horse at first, but certainly they domesticated it from about 1650 BC.

From about 600 BC the Persian Empire dominated the West, and the Persians bred horses which they could use in their activities as undisputed masters of the cavalry. Xerxes, King of Persia (485–465 BC), commanded no fewer than 80,000 chariot and ridden horses in his formidable army. Although the Greeks could not hope to rival the Persian's military strength with the horse, they nevertheless focussed great attention on horsemanship. The Greek historian, Xenophon, wrote texts on hunting, estate management and horsemanship in 360 BC which indicate the degree of interest. From the time of Xenophon to Alexander the Great 336–323 BC), crossbreeding developed, notably with the interbreeding of the Bactrian horse and the indigenous Macedon-Tarpan type.

It was largely warfare and the desire to conquer foreign lands that first created a role for the horse and, second, ensured its migration and survival in other lands.

By the third century BC the Chinese had brought their cavalry force up to about 8000 – initially Mongolian ponies but later a stronger type better suited to the demands of battle which had been bred from imported Niceans. The Chinese went into battle against the Huns who were similarly mounted.

The early history and evolution of the horse is as much the story of nations in conflict. Although journeys of exploration and the exchange of gifts between the reigning monarchs or as wedding gifts accounted to some extent for the introduction of the horse in every land, it was nevertheless battle that required the horse – and in very substantial numbers. As wild horses continued to be captured and subsequently bred, perceptibly different strains started to appear. Even in the first centuries of the Christian era, however, it was realized that certain types of horse were suited to particular sorts of work. Generally, there were two basic types of horse: the finely built, more excitable "warmblood" used in battle and the calmer, sturdier "coldblood" used on farms for all sorts of draft and pack work. The requirement for battle horses

continued for many centuries to come, with its zenith perhaps in what is known as the Age of Chivalry when cavalry mounts had to be extremely fast moving and capable of tremendous endurance over long periods when they were ridden by knights in full cavalry armor.

Between the eleventh and the thirteenth centuries the Christians of western Europe made a series of expeditions, the Crusades, to recover Jerusalem and the Holy Land from the Moslems. For the first time the Arab horses were contrasted with the much heavier European horses. The Arabs were light and very quick, affording their riders superb mobility in battle. Crossbreeding continued apace with the ideal being a fine, light horse capable of exceptional stamina. With the introduction of firearms, however, armor was used less and less and from then it was chiefly the light horses that were used in battle with the heavy types being reserved for farm work and transport.

Countless numbers of horses by this time had been taken from the wild and gradually their numbers dwindled. It is thought today that only one truly wild horse remains – the Przewalski wild horse of Mongolia. However, every continent today has what are regarded as wild horses or ponies, known as *feral* – those that have escaped domestication in centuries past to return to the wild and roam free.

These pages: **Horses and ponies living free naturally have to be sturdier than their domesticated relatives. Their hair is often coarse and dense for good insulation against a hostile climate.**

> **God sleeps
> in stones,
> breathes in plants,
> dreams in animals,
> awakes in man.**
> Indian proverb

In the Wild – the Natural Horse

For centuries, man has regarded the horse as a loyal and fearless beast, his servant rather than a wild animal free to gallop the plains and moors. Although countless numbers have been taken from the wild, some still do remain. The one truly wild horse, the Przewalski, may be found in the steppes of Mongolia, while other feral types – those that have escaped man's corrals and shelters to return to their native habitat – include the mustangs of North America, the Brumbies of Australia, the Camargue horses of

France, the Icelandic ponies and the Dartmoor, Exmoor, Fell, Dale, Connemara, Highland, Shetland and Welsh Mountain ponies of the British Isles.

The Przewalski

A small herd of a type of horse whose ancestors have never been domesticated still lives today in the mountains between China and Mongolia. The Przewalski stands about 12 to 14 hands high and weighs 550–660 lb (250–300 kg). Its coat is a reddish dun color with a lighter color muzzle and narrow, nearly white rings around the eyes. There is a distinctive dark stripe along the back which continues into the short hairs of the tail. The Przewalski generally has a stiff

Iceland's wild ponies are still an integral part of its rugged landscape. The Icelandic pony is probably descended from ponies brought in by early Norse settlers and later crossed with ponies of Scottish and Irish stock.

mane with short, brushlike hairs. The Przewalski has never been domesticated and remains fearful of man. It is always skittish in captivity and even dangerously aggressive at times, both with other members of the herd and with man. The Przewalski horses in captivity have a special significance in the

evolution of the horse. Some experts believe that the Przewalski is the only type of horse from which all others have descended and that the tarpan was simply a form of the Przewalski, now extinct. Others maintain that it was the Przewalski and the tarpan that gave rise to today's diverse breeds, while still other zoologists perceive the four distinct types described in the previous chapter.

Przewalskis are kept in captivity in a Polish government reserve, in Prague zoo, as well as other, and, through export via Munich before World War II, in New York State's Catskill Game Park. The Catskill herd have not suffered cossbreeding and they generally conform to the accepted type.

Prague is now the center of the Przewalski breeding program, a program not without difficulties. At the turn of the century Frederic von Falz-Fein had imported more than 50 Przewalski foals into Europe for

In the huge expanse of the Icelandic countryside the herds of ponies enjoy the brief summer. In Iceland the scattered human communities rely greatly on these hardy animals. With their help they were able to overcome the inhospitable wilderness, glaciers and lava hills.

The Vikings brought horses to Iceland. In the thousand years since then they have often been forced to scavenge for food. In spite of this they have managed to develop into healthy, powerful animals. The people of Iceland owe much to these robust little horses.

76

a new park at Askania-Nova in the Ukraine (the herd was subsequently destroyed in World War II). Of the 50, many died as a result of poor transit conditions and some were bought by the director of Hamburg Zoo, Carl Hagenbeck, who resented Falz-Feins's monopoly.

Hagenbeck unwittingly bought just one foal that was not a pure Przewalski – the mare had been not a wild Mongol pony but a domestic type. The hybrid foal was then acquired by Prague together with most of the others. Unfortunately it turned out not only to be of an impure strain but more fertile than any of the others. The Polish breeders have been beset with throwbacks ever since. Selective breeding, however, whereby those most like the strain are allowed to reproduce, has created the largest herd of the Przewalski horse, maintained by some to be the single ancestor of the horse.

The Polish herd is, nevertheless, clearly valuable for what it reveals of the Przewalski type and its behavior and characteristics.

The Przewalski horse originally lived in sandy, arid regions, often surviving for as long as four days without water in a crushing heat. The horses ate plants for the moisture they contained and drank salty water from the desert soil which they managed to plumb with their hooves. Although the horses in captivity do not have to endure such conditions, their behavior and habits remain largely unchanged. Head of the group is the stallion, constantly on the alert for any sign of danger. If he senses a threat, he will snort to sound the alarm, take a suitable position to shield the herd from attack and charge without hesitation.

When all is peaceful, the stallion keeps a watchful eye on the herd from about 25 ft (8 m) or more away, constantly circling and keeping his charges together. The king of the herd frequently bites and nips the foals and mares to keep them moving. For this reason it is essential that the Przewalski horses

Above: **A solitary mustang seeks shelter.**

Below: **These are domesticated horses, now turned
wild, in the Peruvian Andes,
wandering far away from all
civilization.**

are kept in large enclosures; otherwise an over-zealous stallion is
likely to cause injury. The dominance hierarchy is perhaps best illustrated at feeding time: the mares
with foals are first, followed by the
older colts and fillies, and then by
the older mares. The stallion stands
to one side but, as soon as he
moves in to eat, the herd parts and
waits.

The horses perform mutual grooming rituals which not only keep
their coats clean but reinforce the
structure of the group. Grooming
implies rather more than keeping
the coat sleek and clean: this is the
way in which parasites and insects
are removed and it also loosens the
hairs when the horses molt in
spring. Besides rubbing and flicking
the tail in grooming, you will often
see two horses engaged in biting as
a means of killing any parasites and
removing loose hairs to bring a
shine to the coat. One horse
approaches a second with what is
called an invitation face – the
mouth is closed but the upper lip is

Above: **More than two million
mustangs roamed the prairies
of North America just 100
years ago.**

pulled slightly forward. They then
stand head to tail, alongside each
other, each biting and nipping the
other's coat.

The Przewalski horses seem to preserve a seasonal rhythm in their
mating and birth. Most foals are
born in spring or early summer,
between April and June, while the
few that have been born in Australia – in the southern hemisphere –
have been born in September, with
just one exception. The mare carries
the unborn foal for about 11
months, the same gestation period
as for a domestic horse. The Przewalski mare is particularly defensive
and belligerent, however, and will
squeal and kick should anything
approach. The stallion does not
play with the foal in the way bulls
do with calves, but instead preserves
his role as guardian.

The tarpan

The European wild horse, the tarpan, is now extinct, but it was once a
common sight throughout Europe.
The most tarpan-like descendants
of this horse, crossed with domestic
specimens, have been reintroduced
in the forests of Poland. The best
known tarpan is from southern Russia
and Poland, and it was in Poland at

Overleaf: **A lone horse symbolizes the freedom of life in
the wild.**

Below: **The piebald Chinco-teague ponies live on the Chincoteague and Assateague islands off the coast of Virginia.**

the end of the 1870s that the last wild specimen was shot. The significance of the tarpan in the context of the evolution of the horse as we know it today and of wild and feral ponies has already been described. It remains open to speculation whether the tarpan, as the European wild horse, was the European line of the Mongolian wild horse, or whether it was directly descended from *Equus caballus*, the same species as the domestic horse.

The tarpan was a small, heavily built horse of about 13 hands. Its fairly large head sat on a noticeably short, thick neck, which had a stiffish mane. It was usually a mouse-gray color, sometimes more brown than gray, with scattered whitish hairs through the coat. Like the Przewalski, a dark stripe ran along the backbone.

The essential differences then between the tarpan and the Przewalski horse are the tarpan's smaller size, smaller teeth and slightly slimmer muzzle. It had stronger color around the muzzle, where the Przewalski is nearly white.

The last wild tarpan died at the end

Above: **Although not truly wild, the mustang is now identified with the old Wild West and commands the affection of the public as a protected species.**

of the 1870s and the last captive specimen died at about the end of World War I. Since that time great efforts have been made to breed what is most apparently a tarpan type of horse. In Germany, for example, Gotland and Icelandic ponies were mated and the off-spring then mated with the Prze-walski – chiefly for the upright mane, which it now seems that the tarpan did not in any case possess. Some of the resulting descendants from this exercise can still be seen in German and American zoos, but how close they are to the tarpan type is questionable, if only because both Gotland and Icelandic ponies have little tarpan ancestry.

The mustangs of North America
It is unlikely that the American mustang is a true wild horse in the sense of never having been domes-ticated. The mustangs are horses believed to have escaped from the North American Indians and re-turned to the wild.

The horse became extinct in Ameri-ca some 10,000 years ago, and it was not until the beginning of the sixteenth century that the horse reappeared. When the Spanish con-quistador. Hernando Cortés in-vaded Mexico in 1519, he took with him 16 Andalusian horses. These had originally been brought from Spain and were descended from the more ancient types of Garrano, Noriker, Barb or Berber and Arab horse. The Andalusian is today Spain's recognized breed, with a height of 16 hands, a lightish build and sturdy, arched neck. Cortés' 16 Andalusians comprised 11 stallions and 5 mares, and they were of ines-timable value to Cortés in his drive for domination of the Indians. Cortés was naturally concerned to prevent the Indians acquiring their own mounts for use in battle, but gradually the Mexican Indians gathered a mounted force with horses stolen from the invaders. By the 1670s, although there had been no horses in evidence a century earlier, it was reported that the North American Indians – and in particular the Apaches and Co-manches – were extremely profi-cient riders.
The Indians' horses were known as

Above: **Mustangs graze the prairies, constantly on the alert to avoid man's attempts to capture them.**

Overleaf: **Horses in the wild generally observe a hierarchy in which either the stallion or the leading mare heads the group.**

83

Norway's Fjord horse is descended from an ancient breed that can withstand the cruel temperatures of the northernmost part of Europe. Note the stiff mane that is characteristic of its ancestors.

cayuse, but they also acquired what we know as mustangs – from the Indian *mesteño* (stray or ownerless). The mustangs were escapees from the white man's domestic stock, which were in all probability descended from Cortés' Andalusians. The Indians frequently raided the conquerors and stole many of their horses. They showed a natural talent for handling and riding horses, and it was not long before they were able to take revenge upon the enemy. Armed with bow and arrow, they forced the Spanish to retreat, driving them back far into Mexico.

Safely back in the Mid-West with their own horses now, the Indians usually tethered their stock rather than fencing them in. Innumerable horses escaped to live in the wild, and the Indians, rather than attempting to reclaim them, rode south to Mexico to attack the estates of the Spanish and raid for horses and other livestock.

While the Indians ruled the West, the escaped horses were free to live in the wild, more or less undisturbed. Their numbers multiplied and they grazed peacefully together with huge herds of bison. As the pioneers and explorers from the east and from Europe gradually advanced across the Great Plains, however, the Indians, mustangs and bison alike were under threat. Many horses were captured and domesticated, only to be killed on the battlefields of the American Civil War. Some were exported to Europe only to be killed on the battlefields of the Boer War and World War I, while others were killed by American breeders who required the grazing land for their livestock and regarded the mustangs as a pest. With their Andalusian ancestry, one might assume that the mustangs would have continued the breed's characteristics of strength, stamina, soundness and the ability to endure a hot, dry climate with poor vegetation. However, most Indian tribes paid scant attention to selective breeding and any refinement in the breed has been lost, today's mustangs being described as "ugly, runty, big-headed, coarse and vicious". They have, however, retained their speed and stamina.

With preservation of the world's wildlife becoming a focus in the 1960s and a gradual realization that man alone was responsible for the deterioration of the environment, mustangs were adopted by the public as a cause for concern – and even affection as part of the old Wild West.

The professional mustangers had little regard for the beast, exporting the meat to Europe, chiefly for chicken feed and pet food, and it seems only to have been the Indians who managed to break and ride the uncertain-tempered *mesteño*. While the mustang is not a particularly attractive horse, it is worth noting that it has a part to play in the ecological balance. Seeds are dispersed through its feces, for example, and it is useful to the ranchers of the Mid-West by keeping open trails in the snowbound winter months.

Only 200 years ago there were between two and six million mustangs roaming the plains of North America. Some 25 years ago it is estimated that this number had been dramatically reduced to between 20,000 and 30,000, of which 6,000 were to be found in Nevada. By 1970 the degree of slaughter and poisoning carried out by the ranchers in response to the mustangs' predilection for enticing away domestic mares and grazing the land required by the rancher was only too obvious: just 10,000 remained.

The American public recognized that the mustang would become extinct without swift action. The

Above: The horse that lives in the wild pricks up its ears and distends its nostrils at the first sign of possible danger.

Above and overleaf: **Ponies in Munsterland, West Germany photographed (above) in their shaggy winter coats which** protect them from an inclement winter, and (overleaf) after molting in the spring.

Below: **It could be said that the way to a horse's heart is through his nose. When the mare is ready for mating,** **estrogen is released into her urine, the scent of which can be detected by the stallion.**

"Mares yield so willingly to domination by man because their wild forebears always had a despot over them, the stallion. Now they subordinate themselves to the rider or the wagoner and transfer to him their instinct for submissiveness."
Prof. Richard Gerlach

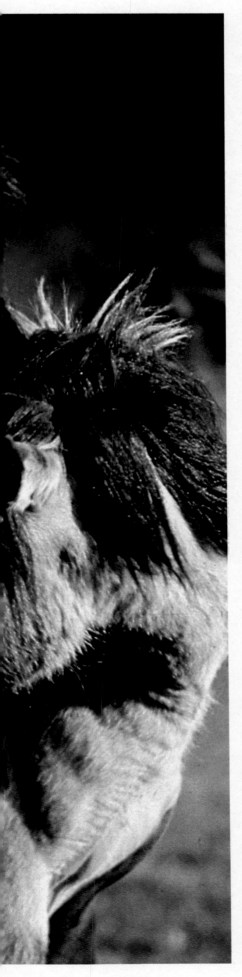

Senate was subjected to heavy pressure to implement laws for their protection – Senator Henry Jackson alone received 10,000 letters in just one week. In December 1971 a law assuring the mustangs' protection was passed, and since that time their numbers have gradually increased, despite action by farmers who claim they are a menace.

The Australian brumby
No truly wild horses have existed in Australia and those that are wild today are from domestic stock which have turned wild. Australia's wild, or rather feral, horses, the brumbies, are descended from the Timor ponies that were brought in from Timor, an island off the north coast of Australia, by European settlers in the late eighteenth century.
The brumbies vary very much in height and are of a fine but sturdy build. They can be of various colors from bay, brown or chestnut through to cream or gray, with a long mane and tail.
It is not known how many brumbies there are, for they tend to inhabit the mountainous areas of Queensland, New South Wales and Victoria. They multiply fairly quickly and when the herds are large, they become a menace to livestock such as sheep and cattle. Ranchers regard them as a pest and regularly round them up for slaughter. Like the mustang, the brumby is sold for pet food.

The gray horses of the Camargue
Nothing is more romantic than the sight of the Camargue horses galloping over the salt marshes, manes and tails streaming in the wind. The Camargue horses are probably the best known of the world's wild horses. Some are broken for the tourist trade, some are used as herding horses for the bulls in local bullfights.
The Camargue gray is usually about 14 hands high and may have descended from Arab Berber stock. They congregate on the marshy lands of the Rhône delta in France, west of Marseilles, and in the 2,000 years or so of their inhabitation, they have become adapted to the soft ground. Their feet are large with hard, flat hooves that distribute their weight evenly.
The Camargue horses have become something of a chocolate-box

stereotype, their hooves throwing up the seaspray as they race at the edge of the waves.

The Haflinger
The feral breed known as the Haflinger is found in the Tyrol. This is now a recognized Austrian breed, bred originally in the Hafling district, near Merano. Some still live in the wild, having escaped domestication.
The Haflingers are thought to be descended from native stock crossed with Arab specimens. They stand at about 14 hands and are of a sturdy build. Normally a chestnut color, the Haflingers have a distinctive flaxen mane and tail. They inhabit the sparsely vegetated hillsides of the Tyrol, but are rounded up at intervals, the best being broken and trained.

The Dulmen
The only native pony of Germany is the Dulmen, which lives in the Merfeld Fault area of North Rhine-Westphalia. As long ago as 1316, the Dulmen ponies were mentioned in the hunting rights of the ruling lord.

Above: **A mare heavy with young in the Merfeld Marsh, West Germany, where about 200 horses live in the wild.**

Their origin is uncertain, but the stock, which may have been akin to the Celtic pony, was probably influenced in its development by domesticated horses that escaped. Since 1850, the herd has been owned by the Duke of Croy, who made over moorland and woodland to ensure their protection. Today's owners are intent on preserving the small herd and have introduced numerous stallions of similar descent. These stallions stay with the herd from May through the summer and are then removed. The stallions selected have included Exmoor ponies, Koniks and Huzules. The Dulmens are very hardy and even-tempered. They live completely wild until, in the autumn, the yearlings are rounded up and auctioned, after being branded with the arms of the Duke of Croy to indicate their origin. The rest of the

herd is then turned loose to return to the wild, with the remaining young stallions searching for a lone mare or, preferably, a herd from which he can oust the ruling stallion.

Other wild horses
Apart from the feral mustangs and brumbies and the ponies of the British Isles, there are at least a dozen other types of wild horse dotted over Europe and South America. The Argentine pampas, for example, are host to feral horses which are regularly broken; they are not thought to be suitable for riding

This page: **The foals seldom stray far from the mare, who will defend them ferociously if necessary. Young foals are often skittish and enjoy playing with one another.**

and are usually put to work on farms instead.

In Europe there are the wild stud farms in the mountains of Sardinia, where the lightly built, tough Achetta ponies live. These ponies are thought to have descended from Numidian horses and have probably lived on the island for over 2,000 years.

Very small herds of feral ponies and horses can be found in uninhabited areas of Sweden, Iceland, Yugoslavia and Peru. Less is known about these small herds as a result of their inaccessibility and the consequent difficulties of reclaiming them from the wild for use as mounts or for draft and farm work.

The British Isles
Native British ponies have become sought after the world over for their qualities of stamina and their suitability as mounts once broken. There are five types found in England, two Scottish, one Welsh and one Irish.

Exmoor ponies
Of all Great Britain's native breeds the Exmoor pony is the most pure, having resisted man's efforts at crossbreeding. These small, hardy ponies seem to thrive on the deso-

late highlands between Devon and Somerset, an area of national park status populated with red deer and sheep.

The origins of the Exmoor pony are a matter of dispute. Some experts maintain that they are descendants of native wild ponies and even consider the Exmoor to be the only pure-blooded wild horse. The majority, however, hold that the ponies are the offspring of escaped domestic stock and so regard them as feral, rather than wild. Fossil deposits dating back some 100,000

years have yielded remains of ponies remarkably similar to the Exmoor, supporting the theory that suggests an ancient ancestry for this horse.

Although there are some ponies on Exmoor which do not conform with the standard type, the Exmoor breed is quite distinct. The height for a stallion is not more than 12.3 hands, while that for a mare is 12.2 hands. One of the breed's distinguishing features is its mealy muzzle, which is an oatmeal color. This light color is also seen around the eyes, inside the ears, inside the legs and on the underside of the belly. Exmoor ponies generally have a wide forehead with quite prominent eyes known popularly as

"frog" or "toad" eyes. Despite their slightly hooded effect, the eyes are soft and warm, an indication, perhaps, of the temperament of a pony which is highly regarded as a child's mount.

Exmoors are capable of extreme endurance, a characteristic which is apparent in the build of the pure type. They generally have a deep, wide chest with a medium length back and powerful hindquarters. Their build is such that local farmers often ride them when rounding up sheep and hunting. This small pony can carry weights far in excess of what their size would indicate.

Exmoor ponies are usually bay, brown or dun, and occasionally gray or black. The purebred type has no white markings on the coat. The coat itself is quite distinctive, being tough and springy. In winter it looks dull, but in summer it is glossy with a close, tight look. The Exmoors are all privately owned, despite their wild existence, and every autumn they are rounded up for inspection and selection in what is known as the drifts.

The Exmoors are often used as foundation stock in crossbreeding when they are mated with thoroughbreds, for example (see Chapter 4), and the foals then inherit the most desirable characteristics of both breeds.

At other times of the year, the Exmoor ponies live as wild horses in herds led by a stallion with about 20 mares. The herds observe the same sort of social organization as the Przewalski horse, already described.

Foals are normally born in May and they are distinguished by their top coat of long, tough hairs which pro-

Above: **The greeting ceremony of two foals in the Merfeld Marsh in West Germany. It is a friendly, benevolent gesture.**

In the unspoilt area of Dulmen Marsh in West Germany, the wild horses still live almost undisturbed by man.

Below and right: **Horses can express a variety of moods. Here a relaxed mouth indicates he is at ease, probably neighing in communication with the others.**

tect them from the inevitable rain of the English climate. Underneath these guard hairs is a thick woolly undercoat. Once the ponies are broken and trained, their patient and equable temperament makes them suitable as children's ponies.

Dartmoor ponies
The Dartmoor ponies, as well as the Exmoors, make excellent mounts for children, for they are good natured and surefooted. The head is usually held high, which makes the child feel safe since there is plenty to hold on to in front of the saddle. Dartmoor's windswept, bleak slopes and granite rocks and tors have been the home of small, tough ponies for centuries. The Dartmoor pony is less pure than the Exmoor, however, and the type varied considerably until 1899, when the first Stud Book was opened. The standard has changed little since, and demand for the ponies is such that they are now exported to

Canada, the United States and most parts of northern Europe.
Somewhat smaller than the Exmoor, the Dartmoor pony stands at a maximum of 12.2 hands and is bay, black or brown. There are also many grays, but no piebalds or skewbalds. The head is held high on a strong neck and the back and hindquarters are powerful and well covered with muscle. The ponies owe their surefootedness to well-shaped, tough feet which have evolved to cope with the typical terrain of the moors.
Dartmoor was a military training area during World War II, and the ponies suffered as a result. Their numbers decreased significantly, and Shetland ponies were subsequently introduced, accounting in part for the variation of Dartmoor's wild ponies.

New Forest ponies
The woodland area of Hampshire was declared a royal hunting forest

some 900 years ago by King William II, William Rufus, and from that time it was known as the New Forest. While hunting in the Forest on August 2, 1100, William Rufus was fatally wounded by an arrow. Native ponies lived in the forest many years before William Rufus made it crown property and, although the origin of the New Forest pony is uncertain, it seems likely that they were similar to the Exmoor and Dartmoor ponies. The New Forest ponies are less pure than any of the other mountain and moorland breeds; Arabs, Thoroughbreds and Galloway stock are among the many to have been introduced. Although this makes it more difficult to establish a standard, it has resulted in a type that makes an excellent ride, particularly for children. The ponies are not only tough and hardy, but very manageable and even-tempered, and, with their narrow withers, comfortable for the smallest child.

At the turn of the century it was felt that while the mares were excellent, the stallions could be improved. Stallions from mountain and moorland breeds, such as the Highland, Exmoor, Dartmoor and Welsh, were introduced to improve the stock. This was an obvious course since native British ponies are thought to have common ancestors. Some years later, however, the larger Arab and Hackney stallions were added. This had the effect of weakening the type, for these breeds were not as hardy and, naturally, it caused considerable variation in size.

The height limit for a New Forest Pony is 14.2 hands but, with such variation, there are two accepted types. The smaller, child's pony is a maximum 12.2 hands and the heavier pony up to 14.2 hands. The ponies can be of any color, and the only variations that are excluded from the standard are piebalds and skewbalds.

Above: **Curiosity is one of the basic characteristics of the horse.**

The herd will move off quickly, staying close together at any sign of danger.

Below: **There are horses which have always been linked with romantic ideas of adventure. One of these is the Camargue pony, that half-wild breed of pony found in the marshlands of southern France.**

The New Forest ponies are exported all over the world, notably to the United States, Canada, and parts of Europe including Denmark, Sweden, Holland and France. The ponies are rounded up in the autumn drifts and inspected and selected. They are again inspected in the spring, when inferior stallions are withdrawn from the herds. With this sort of control, they are clearly not wild ponies, but ponies that are native and which, with a considerable supervision by man, live and breed in the wild.

The Dales ponies
The Dales pony is a native of the Yorkshire Dales, particularly on the eastern side of the Pennines. It is a large, fairly heavily built pony and its capacity for pulling heavy loads made it indispensable to the local farmers.

In addition to heavy farm work, the Dales ponies were also used as draft and pack animals by traders and by the lead miners of Northumberland and Durham.

The Dales pony is probably descended from the ancient Celtic pony, the stock being crossed with Galloways and Welsh cobs.

Their powerful frame, good temper and surefootedness made them suitable as pack and farm ponies. They look rather like carthorses in miniature, with their characteristic fine hair around the heels and feet. Dales ponies can be of any color except gray, usually being black, brown or bay.

With twentieth-century mechanization, the Dales pony has been superseded by the car and other forms of transport for farm work, as well as by machines in the mines. By the 1950s it began to look as if the breed would die out, but fortunately the pony found alternative roles – in ponytrekking and harness-work. Today its future is assured, with demand far outstripping supply.

The Fell ponies
The Fell pony comes from the same stock as the Dales pony, and is very similar in appearance. They are native to the fells of the Lake District and, like the Dales pony, were bred by local farmers for all types of farm work. They were also sold as pack ponies in the lead mines and for all sorts of draft work in the neighboring industrial areas. Its equable temperament made it very suitable as the all-purpose pony on the farm – not merely as a draft animal, but as the shepherds' mount and the family trap pony. Fell ponies are a maximum of 14 hands with very sturdy legs, a compact body and deep girth and a head well-held on broad, sloping shoulders. They are usually black, brown or bay and occasionally gray. Stallions in particular have been exported to North America, parts of Europe and Pakistan, being particularly valued for the breed's chief characteristic of strength combined with a gentle temperament.

This page: **The Camargue ponies find enough to eat in the fertile areas around the marshlands and small rivers of the Rhône delta.**

The Welsh mountain pony

Wales has four accepted breeds of ponies and horses today, but only one, the Welsh mountain pony, can be said to live in the wild. Confusion sometimes arises between the four types because of the similarity of the names. The other three are the Welsh cob, known as a breed by the fifteenth century; the small Welsh pony of the cob type, which is similar in many respects to the Welsh cob; and the Welsh pony, which is a breed produced by crossing the small Welsh cob with the Welsh mountain pony.

The Welsh mountain pony is one of the most endearing of the mountain and moorland types and it has roamed the Welsh mountains and hills for thousands of years, just as its ancient predecessors had done. They are adapted to a treacherous terrain in that they are very agile, surefooted and move quickly and easily. This freedom of gait makes the Welsh mountain pony, together with its gentle disposition, a superb child's pony.

The Welsh mountain pony stands at a maximum of 12 hands and can be almost any color through gray, brown or chestnut to include bay, black, brown, chestnut and roan. Only piebald and skewbald are excluded. The ponies were traditionally used by farmers and shepherds and in the old Welsh pits. Today, however, they are used chiefly as children's mounts, for riding, showing and hunting.

Above: Camargue ponies have a fairly heavy head, which nevertheless often displays oriental nobility.

The Shetland ponies

The smallest of all the ponies living wild in the British Isles, the Shetland is renowned not only for its size but its great strength. The smallest Shetland pony recorded stood 6.2 hands, the maximum being 10.2 hands. Yet these small ponies with their broad chests and powerful hindquarters made many of them ideal for draft work in the coal mines of the north-east of England in the nineteenth century.

The original ancestors of the Shetland pony may have been of the Tundra type, mentioned in Chapter 1. After the Ice Age, with the introduction of the Celtic pony, Shetlands inhabited the islands from about 2,500 years ago. They may be related to the other native ponies of northern Europe, such as the Icelandic pony and Norway's Fjord pony. At any event, Shetland ponies have lived in the wild for thousands of years, and it is likely that they are of stock domesticated by the early settlers.

The geographical isolation and harsh conditions of the Shetland Islands have combined to produce a breed which is relatively pure and very hardy. Little crossbreeding took place as a result of the inaccessibility of the area and the difficulty of the terrain. With frequent gales and little shelter available, today's Shetland is one of the toughest of all ponies. It is also very intelligent and good-natured. Its qualities made it indispensable in the nineteenth century as a means of transport where no other system was available; the Shetland alone could manage to pick its way over the difficult terrain, both alert and surefooted. For this reason the heavier type was sought after and it was also particularly useful as a pit pony.

The Shetland pony is distinguished by its small size, broad chest and hindquarters, large eyes, small ears and flowing mane and tail. Colors run the entire spectrum from the more common black or dark brown to the less common chestnut, gray, roan, dun, cream, skewbald or piebald.

With the increased mechanization and transport facilities of the twentieth century, the lighter pony is preferred to the heavy type required in the latter half of the nineteenth century. These lighter ponies are greatly in demand as children's

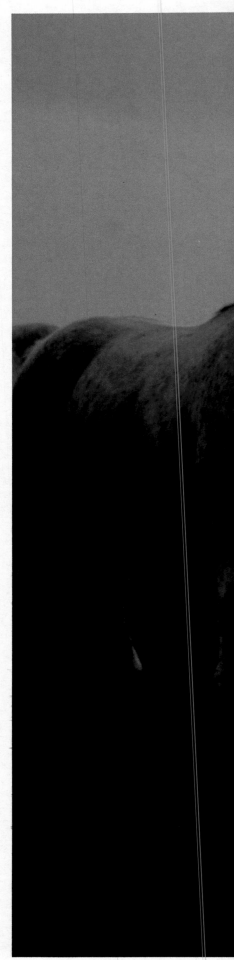

Above: **The Camargue pony is never encountered outside the Rhône delta.**

Above: **The membrane still visible on the newborn foal's hindquarters, the mare starts to lick it gently.**

ponies and are exported all over Europe and, to a lesser extent, to the United States.

The Highland pony

Like the Shetland, the Highland pony is capable of great endurance and shares the qualities of alertness, surefootedness and a gentle disposition. Both types are likely to have descended from the indigenous horse of northern Europe.

The Highland differs from the Shetland, however, in that it is much larger and it is a breed that has been crossed extensively with others. The Highland was found originally on the western islands of Scotland. Over the past four or five hundred years foreign stallions have been introduced, notably French and Arab. The Highland seems to have benefited from Arab blood in that it has inherited the Arab's characteristic loyalty to man.

The Highland pony stands at around 13.2 hands to 14 hands and it is distinguished by a heavy, yet bony build. The eyes are usually large and soft, the ears small and the hooves feathered with soft hair. The ponies on the mainland of Scotland are generally black, brown or chestnut, while the island ponies are often dun with a silvery mane and tail. The lighter colored ponies usually have a dark stripe running the length of the back and sometimes zebra-like markings on the lower half of the leg.

Like the Shetland pony, the Highland was once used extensively for all types of work, but today it is used on farms and for riding.

Below: **The mares in the herd form a circle as the mare is about to give birth, thus forming a protective wall around** **the new life. Primitive instincts command them to protect their progeny, as with all wild animals.**

The Connemara

Like the Highland, much Arab stock has been introduced to the only Irish wild pony, the Connemara. Today there are so few Connemara ponies left in the wild that it is almost misleading to describe them thus. It seems very likely that wild ponies lived in Ireland centuries ago, but the origins of the Connemara are not clear. Today's Connemara, however, seems certain to be the result of the Celtic native pony and crossbreeding, particularly with Arab, Thoroughbred and Spanish stock.

The Connemara stands at about 13 hands and is shortlegged with sturdy shoulders. Almost any colors are seen, from black, brown, dun or gray to the fairly rare roan or chestnut. The hindquarters are normally quite powerful and this has earned them a reputation for jumping. In addition, the set of the shoulders and a good head carriage have helped the Connemara be much in demand as a jumper, and they are bred specially for this reason, many being exported to the United States.

New life in the wild

Of the ponies and horses that live in the wild, some, like the mustangs, are completely wild while others, like the New Forest ponies, merely run wild under regular supervision by owners and breeders. Whether the herd survives, however, naturally depends on finding sufficient food, withstanding the environment and the birth of new foals to perpetuate the species. Foals are usually born in April or May, except in Australia where they appear in September, after the mare's 11-month pregnancy. Colts and fillies, as the foals are called once they are one year old, are sexually capable at about two years. In controlled breeding, however, they are not used until they are considered mature and fully grown – at about four or five years, when they are known as dams or mares and sires or stallions. In the wild, however, a female can mate as soon as the estrual cycle occurs. The cycle lasts between 18 and 21 days throughout the breeding season, which is normally late winter, spring and early summer. During the estrual cycle, the mare's level of estrogen rises sufficiently for her to come into heat for about five days. During this time, some of the estro-

The newborn baby horse possesses an awkward grace. The far too long, lanky legs still refuse to coordinate completely, but the frizzy stump of a tail is already wagging cheerfully.

The Camargue ponies probably owe their development to the meeting of oriental and Berber horses belonging to the Arabs, who once settled in Spain, together with smaller native ponies.

gen is passed out through the urine. Its distinctive smell alerts the stallion to her readiness for mating. The stallion can mate all the mares in the herd that are ready, and he will ferociously defend his right to do so. Any rival stallion that presents himself will be seen off with much flashing of hooves and rearing up to bite if necessary. Stallions of the light horse type ejaculate 1⅓ to 4 oz (40 to 100 cc) of semen with an average concentration of 1¾ billion sperm per ounce (60,000 per cubic mm).

The estrual cycle culminates in ovulation, the release of the egg, or ovum. If the stallion mates with the mare at this optimum time she is likely to conceive. Although mating can take place in late winter, spring or early summer, horses living in the wild in the northern hemisphere are more likely to mate in May, June or July (or september or october in the southern hemisphere), when the insemination capacity of the stallion and the fertility of the mare are at their height. During these months the stallion repeatedly herds the mares together. He checks regularly the spots where the mares urinate and marks them with his own urine.

Once the stallion gets the scent of the mare's estrogen, it rouses him to a frequent pursing of the lips and as he does this he picks up the scent with the inside of the upper lip. He raises his upper lip, closing the nostrils, while the jaw is shut. The stallion approaches the mare in a visible state of excitement with ears pricked, nostrils flared and neighing with gusto. If the mare does not repel him with shrill squeals, greeting him instead by sniffing at his nostrils, the stallion considers himself encouraged. They circle around each other, sniffing, nibbling and rubbing. Each smells the other's genitals until the mare invites the stallion by turning her back to him and standing with her hind legs apart. The mating can be over in just a minute or two, but it is not unusual for a longer, friendly skirmish to develop.

Pregnancy lasts about 11 months, usually reckoned to be 334 days for colts and a day or two less for fillies. During this time, the mare's belly grows more and more distended until her normally cylindrical body is virtually completely round.

Just before the mare is ready to give birth, her belly will drop and her hindquarters slacken. Between one and ten days before birth her udder will develop, and a wax will form on the nipples.

When the wax drops off the teats, the mare paces around as birth is approaching. The mare will lie down when the labour pains intensify and shortly afterwards the membranes of the bag that contain the foal, the caul, break to release the mare's waters.

Birth usually takes about 30 minutes, and it is relatively simple provided the foal is "presented" correctly with the forefeet and head first. About one per cent have a breech presentation with the hindquarters emerging first, which can be problematic.

In a normal birth the foal's forelegs emerge, followed by the head and the rest of the body. The bag or caul splits as the foal emerges and the mare washes off the rest of it as soon as the foal is completely born. The mare starts licking the foal straightaway, partly to remove the rest of the caul and partly to dry the foal, to get its circulation going and to reassure it.

The newborn foal, still wobbly, will attempt to stand up almost immediately to search for the teat. The umbilical cord, which supplied food to the foal before birth,

Above: **Threatening gestures play an important part in establishing and maintaining the order of rank among horses that live in the wild.**

breaks at this point and the mare then cleanses herself of the afterbirth. The foal will suckle for a short time and then sink exhausted to the ground with his mother. Within a few days the foals are playing with each other, although they still stay close to the mare. Foals generally double their birth weight in the first month and triple the birth weight by the end of the second month.

Without man's intervention, breeding in the wild would take its natural course: the breed would remain pure and only the fittest would survive. Exceptionally tough ponies would probably result, but there would be no infusion of qualities alien to the breed. In many of today's wild herds, however, foreign stock has been introduced and breeding is carefully controlled. In the autumn drifts in the New Forest, for example, inferior animals are withdrawn so that they do not breed the following spring. A breed can be greatly improved by introducing stock that possesses the qualities that the indigenous horse lacks.

Social order in the wild

The wild horse's first instinct is to deflect attack and preserve his freedom. Even quite young foals will bite and squeal or kick if approached – and the mare will provide quite aggressive support if there is a real threat of danger. Wild horses are constantly on the alert, pricking their ears forward to listen and distending nostrils to catch the scent of any intruder. If attack seems imminent, the horses' ears are laid back and they will usually bolt, with the stallion positioning himself between the herd and the potential enemy.

As far as the reigning stallion is concerned, any other stallion presents just as much of a threat as man or a would-be predator. He will face his rival with arched neck, head well forward and attack. The fight can be a bitter one, for the intruding young stallion has to find his own herd and achieve dominance as part of his natural drive to reproduce. A young stallion will sometimes find unaccompanied fillies which have been driven off from their original herd by the stallion as soon as they are old enough to mate. If, however, the young stal-

These pages: **In every horse there is a fiery soul. These two rivals rear up high, strike each other with their front hooves and snap at each other's necks and flanks.**

lion does not find a herd without a stallion, he will try to oust an older stallion.

Each herd is a community, and these communities seldom mix with one another. If watering holes are common to more than one herd, one group will wait until the other has finished. Within the community itself, the hierarchy is carefully observed. At a watering hole, for example, the mares with foals drink first followed by and the colts and fillies. Any of them will pause if the stallion breaks in, and wait until he has finished.

Gestures and sounds are used to maintain the social order, and also by the stallion to give an exaggerated impression of his strength and stamina. In trying to impress a mare who is in season or to deter a rival stallion, the lead stallion arches its neck so that its head is held high with the chin pulled on to the breast. Characteristic threatening gestures include the ears lying flat, the neck low and the head outstretched, with the whites of the eyes showing. Snorting often denotes a warning signal, while neighing is more likely to show friendly intentions.

A close community with a leader and an established order of rank has certain advantages in that feeding grounds are shared and a predator is less likely to make a successful attack on a herd than on a solitary animal. Although there are now few predators, the horse's watchfulness is the evolutionary response to the predators that roamed the plains and moors centuries ago.

The horse's order of rank is partly what has accounted for man's great success in domesticating the horse and the closeness of the relationship between man and horse for thousands of years. Once man has captured the horse and imposed his own will, the horse's natural sense of a hierarchy takes over. The horse, too, is an innately trusting animal with a somewhat subservient nature, so that once it is broken and trained it will become the servant man wishes it to be.

Two stallions lunge at each other, their teeth bared and try to grasp and tread down the rival. If the weaker goes down, the stronger will hold him there and may rip his coat with his teeth. If the loser fails to release himself from the strangle-hold, the duel can even end in death.

Introduction by

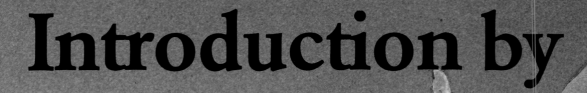

Dorian Williams

**Equestrian commentator
for BBC Television since
1951 and author of many
books on all aspects of
horses and horseback riding.**

The partnership between man and
horse has been of crucial significance
to the course of history. It is to the
horse that we owe not an incon-
siderable part of our civilization.
Until about 5,000 years ago the horse
was to man nothing more than a
provider of meat. There is evidence
that around 3,000 B.C. horses were
being domesticated in China and
Asiatic Russia. Once the value of the
horse was appreciated, its use,
especially in war, was quickly
extended to all civilizations. Mastery
of the horse as a chariot-puller and in
cavalry became vital factors in the
creation of Empires. In almost all
great exploits and achievements up to
the beginning of the 20th century the
horse had its role to play. It is today
difficult to realize how important the
horse was to man in history.

Dorian Williams

The muscle power of the horse has provided man with transportation, the means to farm more efficiently, clear the forests, herd cattle and countless other roles. No wonder that in some cultures horses were revered as a God or invested with magical significance.

The horse has been immortalized in all forms of art. It is, however, interesting that the horse is generally seen as a servant to man. It should not, however, be forgotten that the horse, despite centuries of domestication, has still the primitive instincts and desire for freedom. History has not always treated horses well. The role of the horse today in most countries is one centered on sporting and leisure activities. We have the chance now to appreciate fully the horse for its own sake, and not for its traditional role as a beast of burden and an instrument of war.

Dorian Williams

The Horse in History –

the Great Contribution

Man's success in domesticating the horse is such that the history of the horse is as much the story of military conquests, new alliances and altered frontiers as it is part of the history of agriculture, industry and transport. The evolution of the horse would not have followed the path it did without man and his insatiable desire for seizing new lands and conquering nations, nor would man have achieved these successes without the horse.

The story is not entirely one of warfare, however. The horse proved to be a loyal and willing servant with a faith in human beings that they themselves might find hard to justify. Immensely strong and intelligent, the horse was put to work on farms and later, in mines. Horses played a decisive role in the development of agriculture and industry and in transport, too, when coach and carriage were the only means of overland travel.

The great beauty and power of the horse has raised it far beyond the level of a functional animal in the human imagination, and the horse has become an integral part of many cultures all over the world and part of ancient mythologies. The horse's grace and heroism has found a place in all the arts.

Below: **Ancient mosaics evidence that the horse was domesticated by man early in history.**

The early rulers

Primitive man used the horse only for food, but it was gradually realized in many different parts of the world that horses could be captured and tamed to great advantage. By about 3,000 BC horses were ridden and harnessed by the Chinese, who learned their skills of horsemanship from invading tribes. Pitched battles involving huge cavalries were not infrequent. The chariot in battle would

have been a familiar sight in many parts of the world, with the Persians, for example, toppling rulers far and wide in the seventh century BC, using chariots as well as cavalry.

By 3,000 BC the horse was domesticated in many parts of Asia, Europe and North Africa, and in Greece by about 2,000 BC. The Greeks, like the Egyptians before them, heralded the beauty and grace of the horse both in literature and in art. Mosaics, wall paintings and vases survive to this day to testify of the horse's role in the ancient world. Greek mythology tells of the creation of the horse by the god Poseidon. As the offspring of the god of earthquakes, the sea and of horses, the Greeks revered the horse. They believed that unusually beautiful foals would result from a conception that had been accompanied by the music of flutes, and so they played songs of marriage to their horses.

The Romans too realized the value of the horse in military conquest. With Spain, Sicily, Sardinia, Corsica and North Africa under control, they used the horses captured in these lands to conquer the Greeks. Julius Caesar quickly saw the need for possessing an invincible cavalry and, after the failure of his initial attack on Britain, he returned in 54 BC with a cavalry of 2,000, using horses 15 hands high against the Britons' horse-drawn chariots. Political expansion and the desire for prestige, both military and social, carved a special place for the horse, the effects of which are complex and far-reaching. Suffice it to say that Britain would not have the road system it has today, for example, had it not been for the Romans and learning all over the

Left: **Man has traditionally respected the horse's strength, and here the great beauty and power of the horse is embodied in sculpture.**

world would have been infinitely much slower without dispatches by the horse.

As learning and scientific knowledge slowly started to take root, mythological tales and beliefs became fewer. The horse continued to be revered, however, and a reminder of the Saxons' invasion of Britain remains to this day: the white horse carved on England's chalk downs is reputed to be the ensign of the Saxons.

The age of chivalry

Chivalry – from the French *chevalerie* or horsemen – was the name given to the era that began in the tenth century and saw the knights and fighting noblemen of Britain engaged in many a bloody skirmish. That chivalry has attained its present-day meaning reflects the characteristics of the ideal medieval knight: courtesy, honor and a commitment to protect the weak. During this period the horses of the cavalry were required to be able to carry into battle a knight in full armor, weighing as much as 500 lb (230 kg). That a cavalry existed at all and that there were heavy horses in Britain is attributed to the Norman invasion of 1066, when William of Normandy commanded his 14 hand horses at Hastings. Until this time England had no cavalry, but these heavy horses were bred and we can see their descendants today in the Percheron and the Shire. Wars all over Europe and North

Africa were fought on horseback, the Crusades affording the opportunity of crossbreeding the light Arab horse with the heavy English horse. Without horses, the flowering of European knighthood and chivalry is inconceivable. With the introduction of firearms, however, military tactics relied less on the charge, with knights wielding the sword and the spear, and more on guns. Since this meant that the cavalries no longer had to make such close contact, armor became unnecessary. Consequently, lighter horses with a greater agility were preferred to the heavy horses, and from the sixteenth century the cavalry concentrated on reconnaissance with swift light horses.

The Red Indians

While the age of chivalry reached its peak in Europe, the Plains Indians of America were acquiring considerable powers of horsemanship. Most of the 400 or so tribes were long-legged, but the Comanches, in particular, were a short-legged people who seemed more at home on the horse than on the ground.

The Mexican and American Indians were originally descended from the Mongol peoples, and they inherited the Mongol expertise in horsemanship. For mounts they raided the white settlers in Mexico, although they sometimes took feral horses from the wild. The horse had earlier become extinct in

Below: **A commemoration of the sixth century B.C. four-horse chariot races at Olympia in Greece.**

the Americas, but with the arrival of Cortés, the Spanish conquistador, in 1519, Coronado, and De Soto in 1539, horses were seen once again. These Spanish explorers and adventurers were masters of Spain's age of chivalry and, in their conflicts with the Moors at home, had learned the value of horsemanship and the cavalry.

Many of the Spanish horses escaped their owners and this comparatively small nucleus is thought to be responsible for the rebirth of the horse in the Americas. Not only did these horses survive and multiply but they formed huge herds in the West, which, clearly,

Above: **The chariot may have been the first way in which horses were used in warfare.**

Below: **The cavalry charge was a prime military strategy for many centuries.**

offered them a terrain and environment upon which they could thrive. The Indians captured the horses and soon started to display unparalleled powers of horsemanship, presenting the white settlers with a formidable force. Whereas the white man was primarily interested in the acquisition of new lands and in exploration, the Indian sought only to preserve himself in the face of the enemy.

The Indians would swoop into battle, fiercely painted, their headdresses fanning out around their heads and increasing their small stature so at one with their horse that they could discharge hundreds of arrows and wield 14 ft (4.3 m) lances without losing control of their steed.

The Comanches were said to be the most effortless riders of all the Indian tribes. American ethnologist George Catlin (1796 – 1872), in his *North American Indians*, wrote of the "exceedingly expert" Comanches: "Amongst their feats of riding, there is one that has astonished me more than anything of the kind I have ever seen, or expect to see, in my life: a stratagem of war, learned and practised by every young man in the tribe; by which he is able to drop his body upon the side of his horse at the instant he is passing, effectually screened from his enemies' weapons as he lies in a horizontal position behind the body of his horse, with his heel hanging over the horse's back; by which he has the power of throwing himself up again, and changing to the other side of the horse if necessary. In this wonderful condition, he will hang whilst his horse is at fullest speed, carrying with him his bow and his shield, and also his long lance of fourteen feet in length, all or either of which he will wield upon his

enemy as he passes; rising and throwing his arrows over the horse's back, or with ease and equal success under the horse's neck…"

The 300 years or so of the Indians' rule on horseback has come to be known as the horse culture. They raced, hunted and fought – attacking every rival they encountered, sometimes with a demon stealth and sometimes with bloodcurdling shrieks – to protect themselves and their lands.

The Indians called their horses *mesteño* – without an owner – which in English became mustang. Those of their descendants that escaped slaughter – either for meat or by ranchers who regarded them as a pest – still roam North America today, but in greatly diminished numbers.

Overleaf: **The Renaissance painter, Albrecht Altdorfer (1480–1538), placed the battle between Alexander the Great and Darius III in 333 B.C. in a medieval setting. The painting was commissioned by Duke William IV of Bavaria.**

Different strains

With the invention of firearms in Europe, cavalries no longer required the immensely sturdy horses that had been capable of carrying knights in a complete suit of armor. Quick, light horses became much in demand and during the reign of Charles II (1660–85) much oriental stock was imported, partly in response to the king's introduction of racing at Newmarket. At the end of the seventeenth century the three oriental stallions believed to be the founders of the Thoroughbred were imported to England. Cavalries started to use these lighter, quicker horses. The horse was to play an essential role in war for another 300 years. In the eighteenth century Peter the Great, for example, took command of a mounted force of 84,000 men; and the dashing Hussars, sabres aloft, galloped into battle on nimble steeds.

Below: **The Mongols invaded China repeatedly with a superb cavalry. In the twelfth century the Mongols had over one and a half million cavalry – the biggest in history. On 13-hand ponies they conquered most of Asia and eastern Europe.**

The Napoleonic Wars

The wars fought by Napoleon I from 1803 to 1815 involved coalitions and alliances between nearly all the European nations. They culminated in Napoleon's defeat at Waterloo in 1815 by Wellington, the Iron Duke, and Blücher, in command of the Prussian forces.

The wars caused inestimable devastation and loss of life, both human and horse, and as was the case in previous wars, the horses of the cavalry formed the main force. Two great horses have been recorded in the history of these wars: Napoleon's light gray Arab stallion, Marengo, and Wellington's chestnut charger, Copenhagen.

Military historians have claimed that Napoleon's earlier successes were entirely attributable to his genius and skill in deploying his huge cavalry. Nevertheless he sustained huge losses, retreating from Moscow in 1812 with his 30,000 cavalry reduced to 2,000 horses. Napoleon's total cavalry numbered about 100,000, with Napoleon himself mounted on a gray or cream Arab or Barb charger. Napoleon is reported to have lost 18 chargers in battle, and Marengo, Napoleon's last mount in battle, was wounded eight times. By the time Marengo saw action at Waterloo, he was 22 years old, but his indomitable courage and vitality remained. Marengo was subsequently taken to England, where he remained until his death at the age of 38 in 1831.

No less a steed was the Iron Duke's Copenhagen, named after the siege of the town in which Copenhagen's mother took part. Copenhagen is remembered for his extraordinary stamina and a spiritedness which apparently made him a difficult ride for all but the Duke. On the eve of the Battle of Waterloo, Copenhagen was fed at 8.00 in the evening, having gone without food for long hours during the 60 mile (95 km) journey carrying Wellington to meetings with his own generals and with the Prussian troops. On the day of the battle, Copenhagen carried Wellington from dawn to nightfall in appalling conditions and considerable danger, his heroism and his energy undeterred. Copenhagen died in 1836 and was buried with military honours. He is immortalized, with the Duke, in Boehm's bronze statue opposite

Apsley House in London's Piccadilly.

The last campaigns

The development of automatic weaponry and mechanized transport in the late nineteenth and twentieth century meant that less and less emphasis was placed on the cavalry charge. Light artillery was still sometimes horsedrawn in World War II, but horses were never again used in battle in the way that they had in the preceding centuries.

The intervening hundred years saw numerous bloody encounters which required the horse for its characteristics of strength, endurance, fearlessness and loyalty. The British fought in India in a series of battles

during the nineteenth century and the early years of the twentieth. The troops had to travel huge distances over uninhabited land, so the horses had to be sturdy, and capable of great stamina. Smaller mounts included the Arabs, while the larger were the Walers from Australia, the result of Arab and Thoroughbred crossbreeding.

The middle of the century saw Russia at war with Turkey, Britain, France and Sardinia in the Crimean

Above: A Chinese painting on silk of Ghengis Khan hunting with a falcon.

The invasion of the Huns under Attila, their nomadic leader from Asia, terrified Europe in the first half of the 5th century. He was known as the "Scourge of God", and for some decades he was the ruler of the then known world.

Emperor Barbarossa fighting the Turks. Battle in the Middle Ages relied largely upon the charge with sword and spear, and the heavily built horses had to withstand a knight clad in full armor.

Below: **Horses in the Middle Ages required sturdy legs and a thickset body to carry a fully armored knight weighing between 440 and 500 lbs.**

War (1853–6), which was caused by Russia's attempt at expansion. The Charge of the Light Brigade at the Battle of Balaclava (1854) was a military catastrophe in which a misunderstood order in the confusion and panic of battle led to the charge. Over 400 horses perished as they charged directly into the Russian artillery some 2,000 yards (1,800 m) away. Tennyson described the appalling incident in his poem, *The Charge of the Light Brigade:*

"Cannon to right of them
Cannon to left of them
Cannon in front of them
Volleyed and thundered...
Into the jaws of Death,
Into the mouth of Hell."

The last years of the horse in military conflicts included those campaigns at which the British Field Marshal, Lord Kitchener, served. As head of the Egyptian army, Kitchener returned the Sudan, out of the hands of the Khalifa forces, to Egypt. Winston Churchill, aged 24, fought hand-to-hand in the decisive battle of Omdurman (1898) near the Nile under Kitchener's command. Churchill later wrote a moving account of the conflict in *The River War* (1899):

"Riderless horses galloped across the plain. Men, clinging to their saddles, lurched helplessly about, covered with blood from perhaps a dozen wounds. Horses, streaming from tremendous gashes, limped and staggered with their riders. In 120 seconds five officers, 65 men and 119 horses out of fewer than 400 had been killed or wounded."

The Boer War, the last of the British Indian campaigns and World War I all saw the horse in action. In the course of the Boer War (1899–1902) Britain lost 350,000 out of over half a million horses as a result of hardship and disease. The tough little ponies of the Boers fared rather better.

Millions of horses were used in World War I, both in cavalries and as draft and pack animals. Losses of horses through hardship and exposure exceeded those sustained in battle by five times. The battle of Verdun (1916) alone saw the death of 7,000 horses. Horses continued to be used through World War I on the Western and the Eastern Front. They were subjected to the most miserable life, sometimes traveling 60 miles (95 km) a day without break for food or water. They were often used on the battlefield until they dropped. After World War I, mechanization gradually superseded the horse and in World War II they were used chiefly as draft and pack animals and for transport, particularly in areas where any other method would have been difficult if not impossible, such as the Burma jungles. What may have been the last cavalry charge took place near Moscow in 1941, when the 2,000 horses and men of the 44th Mongolian Cavalry Division were mown down by the Germans with their artillery.

The workhorse

The horse had been used as a draft animal to pull carts and heavy loads from the earliest times. These were normally light horses, however, the heavier types being reserved for battle. With the introduction of firearms in the sixteenth century and a decreased need for knights to

Above: **As well as carrying a heavy knight into battle, the medieval horse was himself armored with head and chest pieces that sometimes were artistic masterpieces.**

be armored, light horses came into favor as cavalry mounts. The heavier horses were then turned to carry out work in the fields which previously had been done by oxen. Oxen were extremely strong, but speed was not one of their qualities. By comparison the horse was so much quicker, more agile and mobile that eventually it replaced oxen altogether. The last descendants of the heavy horse of the Middle Ages are seen in today's Shire horse and the Percheron. The golden age of the draft breeds came toward the end of the eighteenth century, when more sophisticated agricultural equipment was available to make a fuller use of the horse, and lasted until World War I. After this time mechanization gradually replaced the draft breeds. The draft breeds include immensely sturdy animals, capable of drawing colossal weights, and many have the characteristic feathering of heel and foot that makes the amiable cart horse immediately recognizable.

The heavy horse found a place not only in agricultural work but initially in transport, drawing wagons, carriages and coaches, as a saddle horse, and in industry. Draft horses pulled the early public wagons of the sixteenth century over intolerable roads. The discomfort of the ride is testified by Elizabeth I, who in 1564 traveled from London to Warwick in a large state wagon drawn by six strong horses. It has been reported that the monarch was unable to sit down for a week afterwards. The Queen traveled about the country a great deal, receiving hospitality from her noblemen and subjects. Her journeys were naturally slow and required so many servants that her wagon trains with as many as 400 heavy horses became a customary sight.

As roads were improved in the eighteenth century and carriages and coaches consequently made lighter, so the heavy horse was once again displaced. Lighter, quicker horses were put between the shafts and travel became a more comfortable proposition for many people. Europe, too, had its horsedrawn mailcoaches from the end of the eighteenth century as well as pony messengers. Nowhere, however, was there such a service as the famed Pony Express in the United States. The service ran from 1860 to 1862 from St Joseph, Missouri, through Kansas, Nebraska, Colorado, Wyoming, Utah and Nevada to Sacramento, California. The company had 400 ponies, saddled and ready to depart from the relay stations along the route, thus guaranteeing that the distance of just under 2,000 miles (3,200 km) would be covered in 10 days. The riders would take the ponies at the gallop from post to post to achieve the daily distance of 200 miles – a journey not without its hazards of Red Indians and white robbers. Without the horse, communication within a country would have been nearly impossible. Nowhere was this more apparent than in the huge continents of America and Australia.

Australia had no native horse of its own and the first were imported by the white settlers. Colonialist expansion and the development of parts of Australia in the late eighteenth century and the nineteenth centuries could not have taken place without the horse. By 1918 it was officially estimated that this vast country had a human population of five million and two and a half million horses.

Above: **The Persians of ancient times regarded hunting with a falcon as a distinguished, aristocratic pastime.**

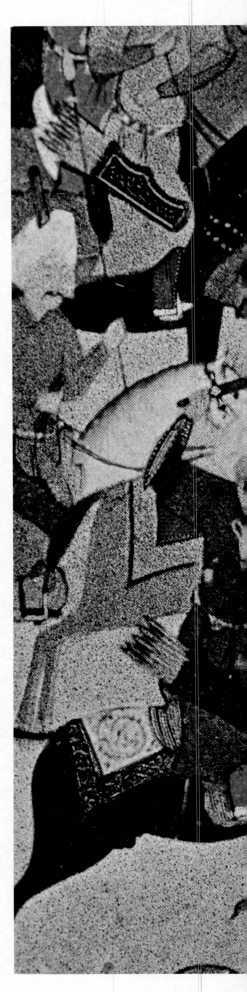

Below: **A fifteenth century Persian miniature depicts the Persians defending their Empire.**

Below: The horse has been revered for thousands of years and has been featured in many ancient mythologies.

Today the ranchers still use the horse in Australia, together with jeeps and trucks. And in America it was reported in 1980 that ranchers found it cheaper and more efficient to use cowhands to drive cattle to market, rather than pay for expensive fuel and have their stock damaged in transit.

The story of the horse in history would not be complete without a mention of the American cowhands or, more popularly, the cowboys.

The cattle herders on American ranches still control and look after the stock on the isolated plains of the south-western United States.

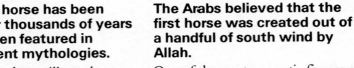

The Arabs believed that the first horse was created out of a handful of south wind by Allah.

One of the great romantic figures of American history, the cowboy has been celebrated in countless films, television series and books. John Wayne was the archetypal hero astride his trusty horse, and *Rawhide* is just one long-running television series popular on both sides of the Atlantic.

The cowboy is no mythical creation. Thousands of cowboys rode the ranges from about the time of the end of the American Civil War (1865) until the advent of a rail system, at about the turn of the century, which enabled cattle to be transported by train. It is thought that there were some 40,000 cowboys at the end of the nineteenth century. The favored mount was the American Quarter horse, so named for its ability to complete the quarter-mile in the minimum time.

The Industrial Revolution saw marked changes in the role of the horse. As a result of mechanization the numbers of people involved in agriculture declined, and many people moved from rural areas to the new industrial towns. Horses were required more than ever for transport, particularly of heavy goods, and for the first time as pit ponies in the mines, a practice that died out only in the 1970s in Britain. Horses were also used in canal systems, although this was later rendered obsolete by the railways. Draft horses, trotting along the tow-paths, were used to pull the barges

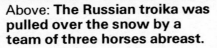

Above: **The Russian troika was pulled over the snow by a team of three horses abreast.**

Below: **A Russian miniature illustrating "The Flower of Stone", a Russian fairy tale, with a stylized horse poised for battle.**

The charge of the Scots Greys at the Battle of Waterloo in 1815. The cavalry at this time was regarded as the prime striking force.

along more quickly by lifting them slightly above the water.

The railways provided an added impetus to the workload of the horse, for increasing numbers of goods had to be relayed from factory to rail depot.

As the twentieth century moved into the motor age, horses were more and more frequently retired or slaughtered. The role of the horse is now confined in developed countries to sport and riding for pleasure and it is probably only a shortage of fuel that will bring it back – as it did in World War II.

The horse in imagination

The horse has for thousands of years had an important position in man's imagination and culture. Man has ascribed to the horse innumerable virtues – strength,

courage and wisdom being some. The horse figures in many mythologies – the Greeks believed that sun was a chariot drawn by horses driven by the God Helios. The role of the horse as a bearer of messages provoked many prophetic ideas such as the Four Horsemen of the Apocalypse of St John in the Middle Ages.

The horse has inspired the creative imagination of men through the ages – in particular sculptors, painters and writers. Sculptures such as the great Assyrian stone reliefs and the Parthenon frieze all bear witness to the man's fascination with the horse. Rodin (1840–1917), celebrated sculptor of the French Romantic

School and his contemporary, Degas (1834–1917), Impressionist painter who also sculpted in wax and bronze, left the world supreme achievements with their sculptures of the horse, a medium which perhaps more than any other pays tribute to the muscular power and the magnificence of the horse. Leonardo da Vinci in his *Battle of Anghiari* presented an overwhelming image of power and fury; revealing the heroic energy and ferocity of the horse. The eighteenth century English painter, George Stubbs, immortalized the Thoroughbred in his paintings. The life of the American cowboy and his horse are memorably recorded in the paintings of Frederic Remington (1861–1909). The latter owed a great deal to the photographic work of Edward Muybridge (1830–1904) in showing the true nature of horse movement. In order to settle a dispute, Muybridge succeeded in demonstrating by means of photography the true nature of the horse's gaits and that there is an instant, when the horse is galloping, during which all four feet are off the ground. Literature has much to say about the horse. The works of Shakespeare are littered with references to the horse and its importance to man. The famous line in *Richard III* – "My kingdom for a horse" has been imprinted on the popular imagination. Fictional writing has created many horse characters from Don Quixote's Rosinante to Black Beauty in the children's book written in 1877 by Anna Sewell which attacks the abysmal conditions to which horses are often subjected. Byron, Kipling, Longfellow and Hemingway are also among the writers and poets who have added to our appreciation of the place and nature of the horse.

In *The Giaour*, Byron paid tribute to the "Blackest Steed" in the lines:
"Beneath the clattering iron's sound
The cavern'd echoes wake around
In lash for lash, and bound for bound;
The foam that streaks the courser's side
Seems gather'd from the ocean-tide: ..."

Above: In the nineteenth century settlers travelled America with covered wagons searching for a new home. Early settlers and ranchers captured many of the wild mustangs then found in the western plains and deserts.

154

Below: **The North American Indians valued their horses, the mustangs, above any other possession. They raced,** hunted and defended their lands from the white man, all from the back of a horse.

The improvement in roads in Europe in the early nineteenth century led to
the establishment of a complex system of coaching inns and staging posts. Travel for
the first time became regular though rather uncomfortable.

156

When man relied upon the horse for farm work, transport and mail service,
every community had its farrier.

Mechanization has replaced this traditional role in most parts of the world. In some farm work, such as harrowing, the horse can, however, still be more efficient.

David Broome

World Showjumping Champion 1970, three times European Champion, five times winner of the prestigious King George V Gold Cup and current holder of the British Professional Championship. Awarded the OBE in 1970.

The first breeds of domestic animals were probably horses – thought to have been in Russia about 3,000 B.C. Today there are more than 200 different breeds and types of horses throughout the world. Man has spent the intervening years in selectively breeding this versatile animal for innumerable different roles. In warfare, farming, industry and transportation different breeds were developed to meet the needs of man. Despite the replacement of the horse by mechanical power, the number and popularity remains undiminished – there are today about 65 million horses in the world. The horse still gives enormous pleasure to mankind – chiefly through its sporting and leisure roles.

It is, however, a constant joy just to observe and appreciate the huge variety of breeds and types. One can see a wealth of different colors, heights, weights, uses – to name just a few of the ways in which horses are classified. Every country has something to offer – the glamorous Hollywood cowboy pony, the Palomino, the tough little Shetland pony, the huge English shire horse to the fast and aristocratic Thoroughbred.

Every kind has its part to play. Man must be diligent in maintaining and conserving this variety. A good number of breeds have become extinct – a loss to the world which can never be replaced. It is to be hoped that all possible efforts will be made to preserve the existing breeds and types for the delight they will bring to future generations. This book with its beautiful illustrations of the horse, in all its guises, strongly puts forward the case for a full and proper appreciation of the horse.

David Broome

Bre

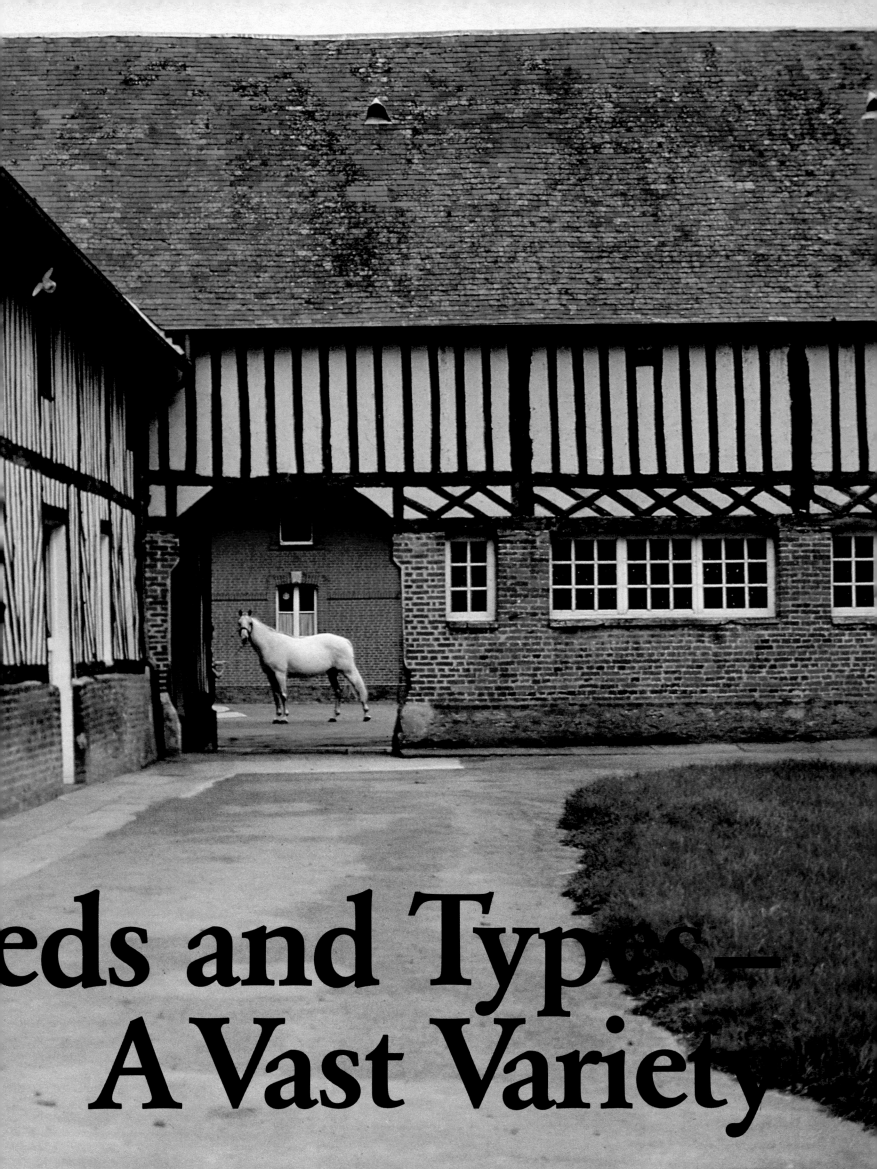

eds and Types—
A Vast Variety

The need to breed horses started as soon as man realized the potential of the horse for farm work, going to war, transport and, in the nineteenth century, industry. It was only the motor age that caused the decline of the "working" horse population. Some third world countries and undeveloped countries still rely on the horse, but in the mechanized West, demand for horses dropped dramatically after the First World War. Increased leisure time has however given horse breeding a new impetus, notably for hacks and for hunters, showjumpers and show ponies. Today there are over 200 breeds all over the world with perhaps another 30 on record that are rare or extinct.

It seems that horses were bred initially from the four main types described previously, notably in the Middle East, Far East and Europe. In China, horses have been bred for thousands of years, particularly the

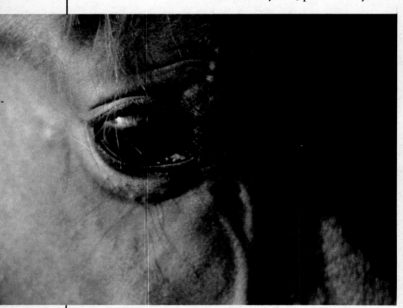

Mongolian Wild Horse. Horses have been bred since the ninth century in Hungary. Poland is the home of the ancient tarpan and although it is now extinct, Polish breeders are attempting to produce the most tarpan-like horse from Przewalski's stallions and Konik mares. The USSR has been breeding horses for only the past 200 years or so, but they have some 40 distinct breeds.

Scandinavia lists among its several breeds the Swedish Frederiksborg, named after its originator, Frederick

II, and the popular Norwegian Fjord pony, known since the time of the Vikings. The base of all French breeds today is the Arab, which the Moors took with them when they invaded France some 800 years ago. Even the heavy Percheron is descended from the Arab, having later been crossed with big draft breeds and Norman horses.

The celebrated Lipizzaner has been bred for many years from the Andalusian of Spanish origin. Spanish explorers and adventurers were responsible for reintroducing the horse to North America, in the

early sixteenth century, and from this small stock evolved the mustangs. From the few horses taken over by the Spaniards, the United States can now boast some 30 breeds as well as a thriving industry breeding European breeds, such as the Thoroughbred and the Shetland, the Trakehner, Clydesdale and Arab.

In Europe, from the Middle Ages and the end of the Age of Chivalry, the coldbloods – descendants of which can be seen in today's heavy draft horses such as the English Shire, the French Ardennes and the German Schleswig Heavy Draft – generally gave way to the lighter, faster warmbloods.

With improved agricultural methods from the seventeenth century, grazing lands were set aside for the horse, a proper diet became available. In tandem with this progress, the horse was needed more and more on the land. As rudimentary farm equipment developed, oxen were replaced with horses on the farm. Different types of horses had long existed but from the end of the seventeenth century owners and breeders practiced selection. Only the sturdiest draft horses, for example, were bred for farm work and the fleetest for battle and hunting. Speed, strength and stamina had probably always been the three chief pre-requisites of the horse,

and serious breeders would attempt to reproduce such characteristics continually. However it is actually height, color, conformation and action in all the gaits that are the distinguishing factors in a breed. Height is normally measured in hands, a hand being 4 inches (10.16 cm). The common abbreviation "hh" stands for "hands high".

Color

There is a wide variation of color of coat even within breeds. Some breeds, however, show a standard color. The Norwegian Fjord Pony, for example, is always dun and the French Camargue always gray. Where the color of a horse is in

doubt, the points (stockings, mane, tail, muzzle and tips of ears) are decisive. The chief colors are black, brown, bay, chestnut, sorrel (US), dun, buckskin (US), cream, gray, roan (blue, red or strawberry), piebald (black and white, and known as pinto in the United States), skewbald (white with any color except black, and also known as pinto in the States) and calico (US, part-colored). Palomino is regarded as a color in European countries, but in North America palomino colored horses are generally regarded as a breed.

Conformation

The ideal conformation in the

abstract really does not exist, for each individual horse's conformation is related to its purpose. Conformation essentially means the skeletal shape and muscle formation, together with the proportions of the two in relation to the whole. Good conformation is essential: if, for example, the legs show a poor conformation the horse is unlikely to have a good natural balance and this will not only affect its gait but probably also its stamina. What the horse is required for is, nevertheless, of paramount importance: the long legs of the racehorse, for example, are not desirable or necessary in the heavy draft breeds, in which

strength and sturdy legs are the principal factors.

The universal breeds

Many breeds are bred in countries other than their place of origin, but there are three breeds which are bred all over the world today and which have a profound historical significance in the development of horse-breeding. These are the Arab, the Barb and the Thoroughbred.

The Arab

Supreme of all the warmbloods is the Arab, from which the English Thoroughbred is descended. Its spirit, grace and vitality have made it one of the most desirable horses

These pages: **Whether bred with man's supervision or in the wild, the newborn foal stays close to its mother for the first few days after birth.**

in history and today it is bred and exported all over the world.

The Arab horse originated in Arabia and was certainly known at the time of Mohammed. With the spread of Islam, Arab horses found their way to Egypt, North Africa, Spain and France, and after the Crusades to northern Europe, notably Britain.

The average Arab stands at 14.2 to 15.1 hh and the most common coat colors are gray (from nearly black to pure white), and also chestnut and bay. Depth of color is regarded as specially important. The Arab's exquisite head with its slightly concave profile is held high. Large eyes are wide set in a broad

vival in arid regions. When the Moors invaded Spain in 800 AD they took Barbs with them. Crossed with indigenous Spanish horses, they produced the Andalusian. Barbs were imported into England by Charles II who used them to improve the speed and stamina of the British racehorse. Barbs have often been used by breeders as good foundation stock, and today Arabs and Barbs are crossed in North Africa to produce riding horses. Barb stallions were ridden by the Algerian cavalry corps under the French. The Barb stands at about 14 – 15 hands and can be bay, brown, chestnut or, less frequently, black or gray.

forehead, the ears are small and the nostrils large and flatting. Hard feet and strong muscles contribute to its quick action. This spirited horse with its fine, silky coat has always been in demand for its great strength, endurance, speed, intelligence and hardiness. When crossed with a mountain or moorland pony, the progeny often makes a superb child's pony.

The Barb
The spread of Islam that caused the Arab to be found in North Africa had a great influence on the Barbs, the horses of northwest Africa, notably Algeria and Morocco. They are very hardy and capable of sur-

The Thoroughbred
The essential difference between the Arab, from which it is descended, and the Thoroughbred is that Thoroughbreds were originally bred solely for racing. Although not as fast as the Arab over longer distances, they are swifter over short distances. Today, "racehorse" is often synonymous with Thoroughbred, and certainly its evolution is almost indivisible from horse-racing.

The recognized breed developed in England early in the eighteenth century in response to the popularity of horseracing and a demand for horses faster than the then British racehorse. All Thorough-

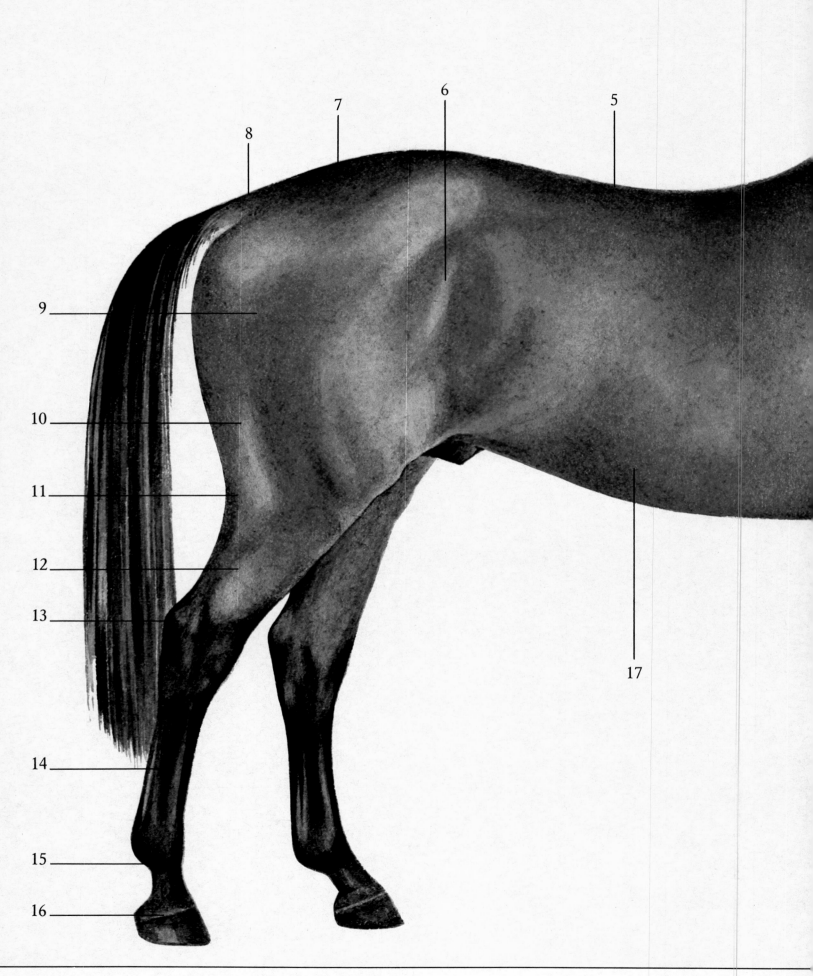

The shape of the horse has developed partly in response to its environment and partly as a result of selective breeding by man. Breeders pay particular attention to the points of the horse and its conformation.

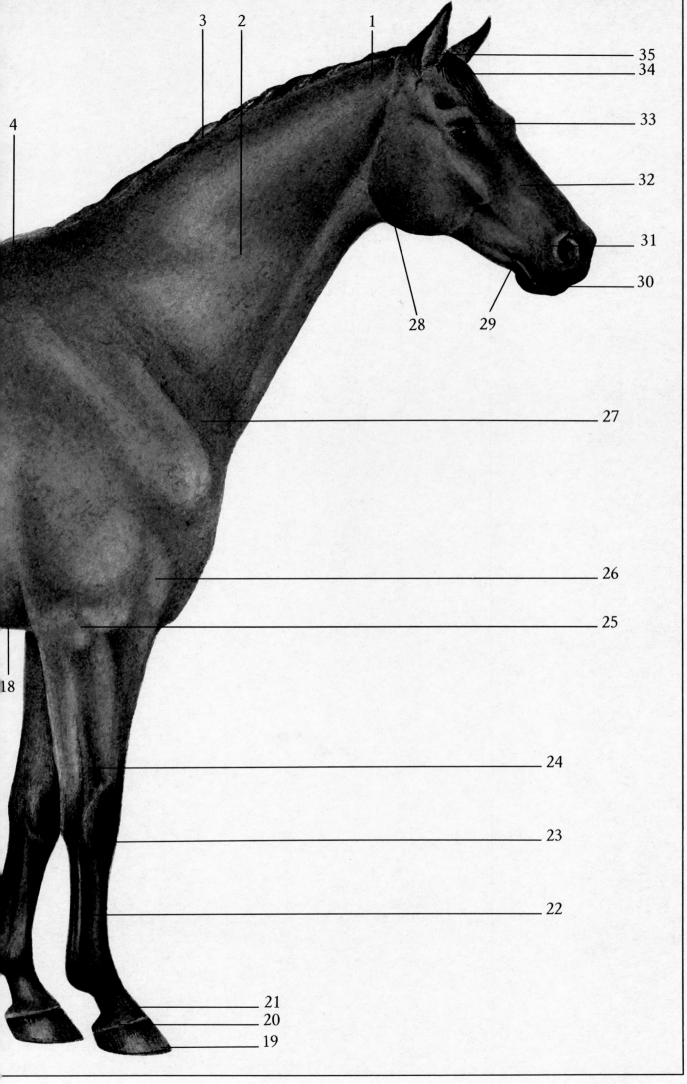

The points of the horse

1 Crest
2 Neck
3 Mane
4 Withers
5 Back
6 Flank
7 Croup
8 Dock
9 Hindquarters
10 Thigh
11 Hamstring
12 Gaskin
13 Point of hock
14 Cannon
15 Fetlock joint
16 Coronet
17 Belly
18 Brisket
19 Hoof wall
20 Coronet
21 Pastern
22 Cannon
23 Knee
24 Forearm
25 Elbow
26 Breast
27 Point of shoulder
28 Throat
29 Chin groove
30 Muzzle
31 Nostril
32 Bridge of nose
33 Eye
34 Forelock
35 Poll

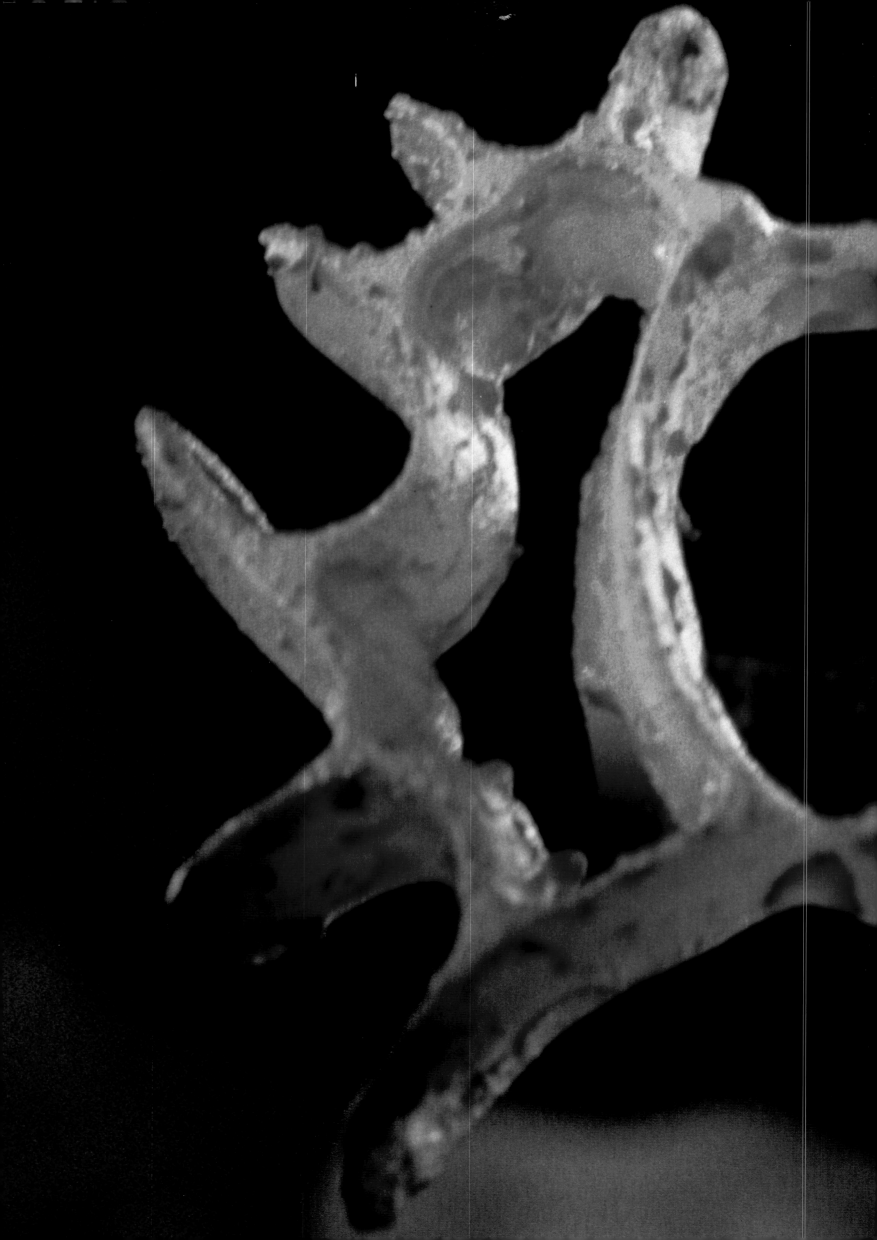

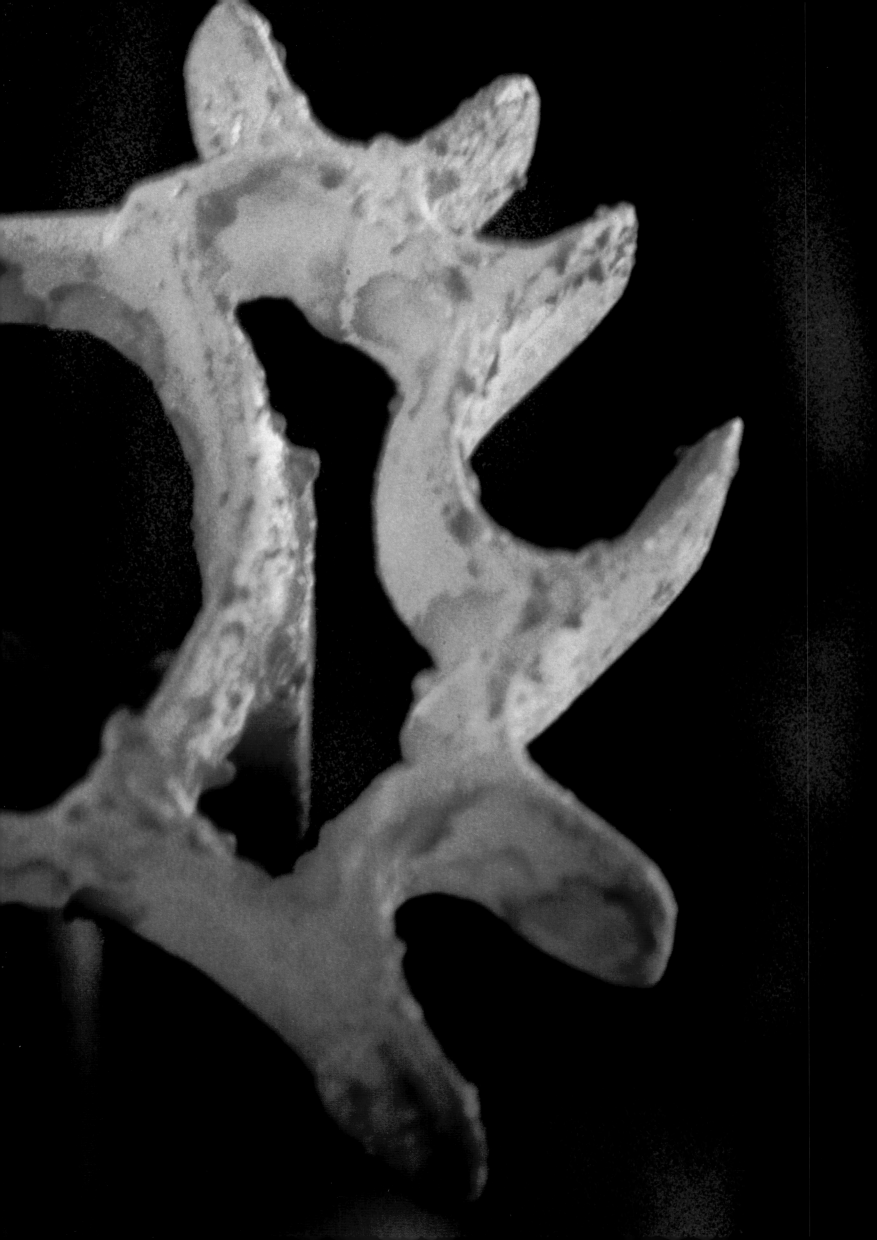

breds can be traced back to the three Oriental stallions, the Byerley Turk, the Darley Arabian and the Godolphin Arabian imported into England in the 30 years between the end of the seventeenth century and the early years of the next. By the second half of the eighteenth century the English Thoroughbred was being bred principally for racing distances of between one and two miles, at which the breed proved unsurpassable. One of the early sires, Diomed, was sold to America in 1798 and, though far from young, established the Lexington line. Lexington himself was America's outstanding breeding stallion for 14 successive years.

Breeding of the Thoroughbred today involves four main types

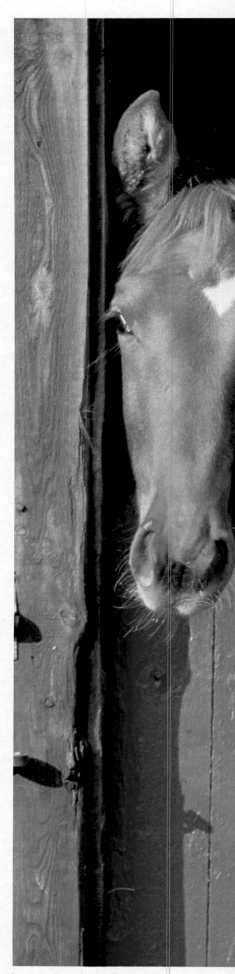

(steeplechasers, sprinters, hunters and hacks), constituting a huge international industry with Britain, the United States, France and Poland at the forefront. America produces the most brilliant young Thoroughbreds anywhere in the world.

The height of the Thoroughbred varies, with an average of 16 hh. Its fine, silky coat is usually black, brown, bay or chestnut – gray being less common. Its fine head with large, intelligent eyes is set on a proudly arched neck into strong shoulders and a deep chest. A short back, powerful hindquarters and superb legs all contribute to the

extreme speed and long, easy action which make it the world's most valuable horse.

European breeds
Europe boasts over 80 different breeds of horse and pony. Nearly every European country can claim at least one excellent breed of horse.

Great Britain
Great Britain is one of the world's horse-breeding centers. The nine native breeds – Exmoor, Dartmoor, New Forest, Welsh Mountain, Dales, Fell, Highland, Shetland and Connemara – are bred and exported all over the world. Britain is also noted for the amiable carthorse, a reminder of the cold-blood, heavy horses of the Middle Ages. These include the Shire – the tallest horse in the world – the Suffolk Punch and the Clydesdale.

The Shire   The draft breeds are noted for their docile disposition and the Shire is no exception. Its gentle temperament and tremendous strength made it invaluable to farmers before the machine age of the twentieth century usurped it. The Shire stands at about 17 hands; stallions weigh more than one ton, and they can pull five-ton loads. Colors are most commonly bay or brown – always with white markings – and sometimes black or gray.

The Hackney   Both Hackney horses and ponies can be traced to the mid-1750s, initially being used as saddle horses and then as light carriage horses. Its vivacious, high-stepping action has caused it to be in great demand for showing and it has been exported to the United States, Europe, Australia and South Africa.

The Cleveland Bay   The old English Chapman mares were crossed with Andalusian and Barb stallions in northeast Yorkshire, some 200 years ago, to produce one of England's oldest breeds. It is used in many parts of the world as a ceremonial coach horse and as foundation stock by breeders of hunters.

The Welsh ponies and horses   The native Welsh Mountain pony has been extremely influential in the development of Britain's hunting and showponies. The American Welsh Pony is a line of the breed. The Welsh Pony (Section B) is the

Previous page and above: **The popular Trakehner breed was established in 1732 in East Prussia. All horses born in the area were branded from 1787** **with a single seven-pointed elk antler brand on the offside thigh. A double antler brand was used on the near thigh for the ordinary East Prussian** **horse from 1888 and their descendants in West Germany are still branded in this way.**

Above: **The elegant Trakehner horses numbered some 25,000 in East Prussia before World War II. Some 1,200** **filtered through to West Germany, where they have been bred ever since.**

A selection of horses from the world's over 200 breeds of horse and pony.

1 The **Anglo-Arab** is the result of crossbreeding Thoroughbreds with Arabs.

2 The **Arab** has been bred longer than any other breed for its elegance coupled with stamina.

3 The **English Thoroughbred** is the supreme racehorse and is bred particularly in America.

4 The **Württemberger** from Germany is a sound, hardy horse of the cob type.

5 The **Hanoverian** horse "Radetsky", shown here, is probably the best known stud bred in Westphalia since World War II.

6 The **Lipizzaner** can be bay, chestnut, or roan but is more often gray.

7 The **Swedish Halfbred**, also known as the Swedish Warmblood, is a first-class saddle horse.

8 The **Kustanair** is a very good draft and riding horse.

9 The U.S. **Palomino** is a color rather than a breed with a golden coat and white mane and tail.

10 The **Missouri Fox Trotting Horse** is named for its distinctive fox trot gait.

11 The **Knabstrup** from Denmark has Appaloosa patterns on a roan base.

12 The **Appaloosa** of the western United States comes in six spot patterns – Leopard, Snowflake, Marble, Frost, White Blanket and Spotted Blanket (shown here).

13 The **English Hackney** with its good legs and springy step is used especially as a harness horse.

14 The U.S. **Pinto**, or Paint, can be brown and white, cream and white or black and white.

15 The **Freiburger** is a cold-blood light farm horse from Switzerland.

16 The **Morgan**, bred in the U.S., is popular both as a harness horse and a saddle horse.

17 The **Criollo** is bred in South America for its strength and stamina.

18 The **Noriker** from Austria is a sturdy, all–purpose work horse.

19 The **Breton** from Brittany, France, is a compact, heavy draft horse.

20 The **Clydesdale** is a heavy draft horse, originally from the Clyde area of Scotland.

Above and following pages: Horse sales, such as this one in Poland, can attract breeders, dealers and potential buyers in large numbers.

result of crosses between the Welsh Mountain Pony and the small Thoroughbred stallion at the end of the eighteenth century. The Section C Welsh Pony or Welsh Pony of Cob type is related to the Welsh Mountain Pony and looks somewhat similar to the Section D Welsh Cob, a larger, heavier version of the Welsh Mountain Pony.

The Irish draft horse and Irish hunter Irish hunters, a type rather than a breed, are exported worldwide, and the draft horse – contrary to its name – is a good riding horse, which, when crossed with a Thoroughbred, produces the excellent Irish hunter.

France
Horse-breeding in France is controlled by the government, which has some 25 stallion depots. France is noted for its young Thoroughbreds and for the Anglo-Norman, the Anglo-Arab and the French Saddle Horse (Selle Français).

The Anglo-Norman This breed is largely the result of the eighteenth-century addition of English stock (Thoroughbred and hunter types) to the early draft horse, the Norman. They were used initially as light carriages horses and as cavalry mounts. Today, they are still exported as cavalry horses and are much in demand for crosscountry, three-day eventing and show-jumping. Both the French Saddle Horse and the French Trotter are descended from the Anglo-Norman.

The Anglo-Arab This is a cross between the Thoroughbred and the Arab and is bred chiefly in France, Britain and Poland. Height varies at around 16 hands and bay or chestnut are the most common colors. These elegant, lean horses are used for dressage, eventing, jumping, hunting and as hacks.

The French Trotter Trotting races were popular in mid-nineteenth century France and quickly spread to other parts of Europe and the United States. Well over 5,000 trotting races are now held in France every year. This lean, lightweight horse of about 16.2 hands – an offshoot of the Anglo-Norman at the beginning of the nineteenth century – is the main breed most used.

The French Saddle Horse (or Selle Français) This is a refinement of the Anglo-Norman dating only from around the end of the 1950s. French Saddle horses are bred with Thoroughbred, Anglo-Arab and their own Selle Français stallions and, to a lesser extent, with French Trotter stallions.

The Selle Français are classified as mediumweight or heavyweight according to their conformation. Mediumweights are more numerous, and the largest of these stand at over 16 hands. Chestnut is the most common color, but may be any color. They are particularly valued as jumpers, having powerful hindquarters.

The Percheron The characteristic docility of the heavy horse is seen in France's draft horses, the Percheron, the Ardennais and the Breton. From Le Perche, Normandy, the Percheron has some ancient Arab blood to account for its grace. It was used in earlier centuries as a war horse, a coach horse and a farm animal. It is especially popular in the United States, where it has been exported since the 1840s, and in Britain where it has been crossed with the Thoroughbred to yield a splendid heavyweight hunter. The Percheron's height varies between 15.2 and 17 hands and it is either gray or black.

Belgium
The notable breed of Belgium are two draft types: the Belgian Heavy Draft which is descended from the heavy Flanders horse of the Middle Ages, and the Belgian version of the

These pages: **The diminutive Falabella at less than 7 hands is bred in Argentina, where breeders tend to prefer Appaloosa markings.**

French Ardennais, the Ardennes.
The Ardennes or Ardennais This
breed is found in the Ardennes
area, shared by Belgium and France.
From the 1600s to the 1800s, the
Ardennes was a lighter breed than
it is today, used mainly as a light
draft animal and during the French
Revolution as artillery horses. Some
of these lighter horses remain but
the Ardennais now includes a quite
massive horse, very thickly built, of
some 16 hands. It is, nevertheless,
an energetic horse and its stamina
and gentle temperament assure its
continuing use on the land. Colors
include roan, iron gray, bay, chestnut and palomino.

Holland
Dutch breeders produce Arabs,
Thoroughbreds, Trotters, Hackneys,
several breeds of pony and its own
native breeds, the Friesland or
Friesian, the Gelderland and the
Groningen, and the Dutch Warmblood.
The Friesland (Friesian) This pure
black horse is thought to have
descended from native horses about
1000 BC. It stands at about 15
hands and is used especially in
harness work. Its use on farms has
naturally declined with mechanization, and even in the nineteenth
century its popularity as a trotting
horse reduced the numbers

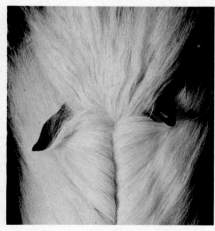

available for farm work.
The Gelderland and the Groningen
These breeds have been somewhat
eclipsed by the development of the
Dutch Warmblood, both of which
have been used in producing the
new breed. The Gelderland is a
good, strong horse with an action
that was very suitable for carriage
work. Usually gray or chestnut, it
stands at about 15.2 to 16 hands. It
has a lot of foreign blood, is noted
as a jumper and is sometimes used
as a light farm horse.
The Groningen was regarded chiefly as a farm animal but is used as a
heavy saddle horse as well. It too
moves with style, suiting it for
carriage work. It was developed by
breeders who crossed the Friesian
with East Friesian and Oldenburg
stock. It too stands at about 15.2 to
16 hands high and is usually black,
bay or dark brown.

These pages and overleaf: **The
Haflinger, which has been
bred in the southern Austrian
Tyrol for hundreds of years,
can be palomino or chestnut**
**with a distinctive flaxen-color
mane and tail. They are long-
lived and very strong, being
used for farm work as well as
riding.**

The Haflinger's original home was the village of Hafling in the Austrian Tyrol and the surrounding country. Breeders have introduced Arab blood, resulting in a very sound pony.

The Dutch Warmblood   A cross between the Gelderland and the Groningen, breeders have sought to establish this breed as a riding horse and jumper.

Denmark
The Knabstrup and the Frederiksborg are two of Denmark's oldest breeds, but their numbers have declined dramatically in the last 100 years. Both have been crossbred and interbred. The spotted circus horse, the Knabstrup, is a result of a Frederiksborg cross. The Danish Sports Horse, a breed only some 20 years old, and the stocky, feathered Jutland are now Denmark's principal horses. The Danish Sports Horse, intended as a general riding mount stands at about 16.1 hands and may be any color. It has been bred from the Hanoverian, native halfbreds, Thoroughbreds, Trakehners and Polish and Anglo-Norman stock.
The Jutland   Normally a dark chestnut with a lighter mane and tail, this medium-sized, stocky draft horse (15 to 16 hands) secured its reputation as a war horse in the Middle Ages when it carried knights in full armor. Its later use as a farm horse continues to a lesser extent today.

Norway
The Norwegian Fjord pony has been known since prehistoric times. Norway's other chief breed is the Døle Gudbrandsdal, also known to have existed for many thousands of years. Not unlike a mountain or moorland pony in appearance, it stands at about 15 hands and is usually black, brown or bay.

Iceland
Riding and all equestrian sports are tremendously popular in Iceland and the principal horse is the Icelandic, many of which live in a half-wild state. They are exported all over the world, with about 300 going to Germany in 1978.

Germany
Among Germany's some 15 notable breeds, the Hanoverian and the Trakehner are of international repute and have both been used as foundation stock for the development of breeds in other parts of Europe and the United States. Selective breeding has been practiced in Germany for at least the past 300 years and is now subject to government control and interest. Imported breeds include the Thoroughbred, the Trotters in response to the popularity for trotting races which exceeds even racing, and the Trakehner – for this breed originated in what is now East Germany. The only pony breed is the native Dulmen, which lives in a half-wild state. Home horse breeds include the Hanoverian, East Friesian, Oldenburg, Holstein, Württemberg and Bavarian Warmblood, while the heavy draft horses – their numbers declining as in most other parts of the world – include the Schleswig Heavy Draft, (a descendant of Denmark's Jutland), and the Rhineland.
The Hanoverian   One of the world's outstanding riding horses, the Hanoverian excels at dressage and jumping and at hunting. Hanoverians have been bred since the sixteenth century, the breed being established in 1735. It was much in demand for 200 years or so as a carriage horse in ceremonial processions and on farms and as a military and transport mount. With the divide of Germany after World War II, Trakehner horses – their

origin in East Prussia – found their way to West Germany and were crossed with Hanoverians to improve them as riding horses. Hanoverians possess much mixed blood in any case, having earlier been crossed with stock of Andalusian descent and with Holsteins and Thoroughbreds.

The Hanoverian today varies in height from 15.3 to 17 hands and can be any solid color. Its energy, even temperament and toughness combined with elegance account for the high prices it commands.

The Trakehner   Thoroughbred and Arab blood was added to native East Prussian horses in the mid-1750s and the progeny formed the basis for this firstclass horse. After

World War II, only about 1200 were transported to the West but breeders have succeeded in producing a splendid riding horse from this small stock.

The Trakehner stands at about 16 hands and any solid color occurs. It is a refined looking horse with large eyes, a small muzzle and sound conformation.

The Oldenburg   At 16.2 to 17.2 hands, this is the largest of the German warmbloods and is an impressive, powerful mount that does well in eventing and showjumping. The breed has been known since the early seventeenth century and it has contributed to the founding of many of the taller saddle breeds. Its own blood is very mixed, having re-

ceived Andalusian, Barb, Thoroughbred, Hanoverian, Cleveland Bay and Norman.

The East Friesian This is related to the Oldenburg, having evolved at the same time with equally mixed blood. The heavy horse becoming outmoded, Arab stallions were brought in after World War II to upgrade quality and make the East Friesian at 15.2 to 16.2 hands a desirable riding horse. Hanoverian stock has been added more recently as well.

The Holstein This breed dates at least to the fourteenth century and, by the seventeenth century, it was being sold to other parts of Europe as a riding horse and a cavalry mount. In the nineteenth century it evolved into an elegant but sturdy carriage horse after the introduction of Cleveland Bay blood. More recently, Thoroughbred blood has been added to achieve the characteristics of the show-jumper and horse trial competitor. The Holstein ideally looks like a first class hunter, standing at 16 – 17 hands. Its traditional colors are bay or chestnut.

The Württemberger Another old breed, the Württemberg, has been known since the sixteenth century. It was initially a strong, thrifty horse used on farms and for other types of work. With the introduction of East Prussian stock with its Thoroughbred and Arab blood, the Württemberger developed into another quality riding horse. The Württemberger is a tall cob type at about 16 hands, and is usually black, brown, bay or chestnut.

The Bavarian Warmblood Originally known as the Rottaler, this breed has been known as the Bavarian Warmblood since about 1960. Always chestnut, this 16-hand riding horse is descended from the heavy warhorse, the Rottaler, with infusions of Thoroughbred, Cleveland Bay and Norman blood, and latterly Oldenburg.

Switzerland

The three notable Swiss breeds all reveal Norman blood. The oldest, the Einsiedler or Swiss Anglo-Norman, dates to 1064 and was much used by the Swiss cavalry and by the French. The Freiburger, also a workhorse, has received infusions of Arab and Anglo-Norman blood and is used on mountains, farms or for riding.

The Swiss Halfbred With less need for the heavier horses, Norman and Holstein mares were crossed with Thoroughbreds to produce a quality riding horse. Trakehner, Hanoverian and Swedish Halfbred stock were all subsequently added to the breed that developed only in the 1960s. Recognized height of the breed is 16.1 hands and any solid color occurs.

Austria

Three world famous breeds originated in Austria and these are the Lipizzaner, used by the Spanish Riding School, the Haflinger mountain ponies described in Chapter 2, and the sturdy draft horse, the Noriker, a descendant of the ancient warhorse of Thessalonica.

The Lipizzaner This justly celebrated breed is capable of quite astonishing feats (see illustration pp. 242-3). The breed is named after the home of the original stud, founded

These pages: **No matter how docile the breed, every breeder and owner is aware of the importance of keeping stallions apart. Their natural** aggression – which is normal behavior in the wild – does not die when the horses are bred in captivity. This is why gelding (or castration) is **carried out. Stallions will fight each other to prove supremacy. It can be a fight of great ferocity with severe wounds inflicted.**

in 1580 at Lippiza near Trieste. The Lippizaner is thought to have descended originally from Andalusian stock, but since then Spanish, Arab and Neapolitan (an extinct Italian breed of Andalusian mixed with Barb and Arab) blood has been introduced.

Italy

Once renowned for its horse breeding, Italy now tends to rely on imported breeds. Horses were bred by the Etruscans more than 2,500 years ago, and the Middle Ages saw the development of the Neapolitan, ancestor of the Lippizaner. Italy's own breeds include the heavy Avelignese pony, its palomino

coloration giving the clue to its relation to the Haflinger, and used for farm work and as a pack animal; the Italian Heavy Draft, a 15 – 16 hand dark chestnut with blond mane and tail, and characteristic carthorse feathering; and the Murghese and Salerno riding horses, both believed to have Oriental blood; and the Calabrese, descended from the Neapolitan.

Spain
The Andalusian   Regarded as one of the most aristocratic of all horses, the Andalusian was officially recognized as a breed in 1571. The breed resulted from the crossing of native Spanish horses with Oriental Barbs and Arabs brought in by the Moors in the eighth century. Spanish monks were largely

Overleaf: **A Haflinger mare and foal on mountain pastures. Note the distinctive brand mark on the mare's shoulders.**

It is an edelweiss – the Austrian national flower – with an H in the center.

Their flaxen manes distinguishing them, the Haflinger ponies stand close together with heads to the center. They stay like this, dozing, sometimes for hours.

Overleaf: **A herd of Haflinger ponies follow the leader past cows at pasture.**

202

responsible for the vigilant breeding of the Andalusian and by the time of Napoleon the breed was desirable indeed. Napoleon's men appropriated many of the best, seriously threatening the survival of the strain. Today the Andalusian is used chiefly by bullfighters and for show purposes. However, it is remembered on two counts: first, that it formed the basic stock for the reintroduction of the horse, via Cortes, on the American continent; and, second, that the courts of Europe in the seventeenth and part of the eighteenth centuries regarded the Andalusian as the supremely noble horse of the aristocracy. This spirited, elegant horse reveals a certain charisma as it walks and, with its high knee action, as it trots. Its popularity was probably rooted in its regal bearing combined with an unusually gentle temperament, even in the stallions. It is usually gray or bay, though it may be black or roan, and stands at about 15 or 15.2 hands.

The Hispano (Spanish Anglo-Arab) A horse derived from crossing Spanish Arabian mares with English Thoroughbred stallions, the Hispano is Spain's chief riding horse, showing aptitude for eventing, jumping, hunting and dressage. It stands at about 16 hands and is usually bay, chestnut or gray.

North America
The American continent had had no horses at all for thousands of years until the 1520s. But today it boasts some 25 light breeds, of which the Palomino, the Saddle-bred and the Quarter horse are perhaps the most famous. American breeds are chiefly top quality riding horses, there being only about six draft breeds. The exceptions are the wild Chinco-teague and Assateague ponies (see illustration on page 82) and the small Galiceno horse, descended from Portugal's Sorraia and Garrano ponies.

Apart from those breeds mentioned above, America has produced the Morgan, the Tennessee Walking Horse, the Standardbred – the world's outstanding harness race-horse and a distinguished trotter and pacer, – the Appaloosa, the Pinto – a color rather than a type – the Albino – the true white horse immortalized by the Lone Ranger,

the Missouri Fox Trotter and, not least, the Pony of the Americas, a recent breed – the result of crossing an Appaloosa mare with a Shetland stallion in 1953.
Canada is noted for its hardy Sable Island pony, a small herd of which lives wild on Sable Island, a thousand miles east of Nova Scotia. Usually chestnut and standing at about 14 hands, they are now used chiefly as riding ponies.

The Quarter Horse Over 1 ½ million of this, America's oldest breed, exist in the United States, and it is popular elsewhere as well and particularly in Australia. It is descended from the Arabs, Barbs and Turks brought in by the six-teenth-century Spanish explorers and subsequently crossed with English horses brought in by the seventeenth and eighteenth-century white settlers. The Quarter Horse was particularly popular with cattle ranchers who valued it for its speed and intelligence. The new settlers bred the horses for their favorite sport of match sprinting – short sprints of up to a quarter of a mile – and from that the breed took its name.

A selection of the world's ponies. Any horse that measures less than 14.2 hands is defined as a pony.

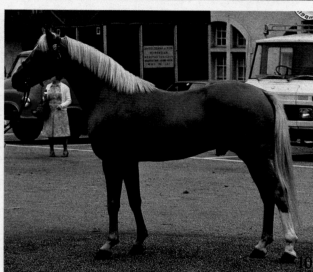

1 The **Shetland** Pony from northern Scotland is a mere 9.3 hands on average.

2 **Icelandic** Ponies are exceptionally hardy.

3 An **Appaloosa** leopard pattern pony.

4 The **Dartmoor** Pony is a first-class riding pony.

5 The **Costeño** Pony of Peru is a variation of the South American Criollo horse.

6 The **Gotland** Pony may be descended from the ancient tarpan.

7 The Greek **Pineia**, standing 10 – 14 hh, is used for pack and agricultural work.

8 The **Welsh Cob** at 14 to 15.1 hands is a natural jumper, a larger version of the Welsh Mountain pony.

9 The **Welsh Pony (Section B)** is a taller version of the Welsh Mountain Pony.

10 The **Palomino** is used for riding, driving and stock work.

11 The **New Forest** Pony of Southern England has Arab, Thoroughbred and Galloway blood.

12 The Austrian **Haflinger**, a sturdy mountain pony.

13 The **Assateague** Pony from the island of that name off Virginia, U.S.A.

14 The American **Mustang** was bred and handled with great skill by the American Indians.

15 The **Norwegian Fjord** Pony has been known in Norway since prehistoric times.

16 The **Pony of the Americas** breed is a miniature Appaloosa at up to 13 hands.

17 The **Hucul**, from Poland's Carpathian Mountains, is believed to descend from the ancient tarpan.

18 Yugoslavia's **Bosnian Mountain** Pony is capable of great endurance.

19 The **Camargue** Pony of southern France is always gray.

20 The **Exmoor Ponies** of Devon and Somerset have a distinctive mealy-colored muzzle.

Appaloosas of the leopard pattern are found in the western United States and exported, particularly as circus horses.

Overleaf: **The Arab is one of the noblest of all breeds.**

These pages: **The Arab horse, found now throughout the world, has been bred by the Bedouins for more than 1,000 years. It is a breed which combines supreme elegance with spirit, fearlessness and loyalty.**

With mechanization, the Quarter Horse, said to be the best for working cattle, was used less by ranchers, but today it is probably the world's most popular horse – particulary for trail riding, showing, dressage and rodeo. It stands between 15.2 and 16.1 hands and although often chestnut can be any solid color.

The Saddlebred   The American Saddle Horse is distinguished by its five gaits: walk, trot, canter, slow gait (a slow version of its fifth gait), and the rack – a stylish, prancing step in which each foot pauses momentarily before returning separately to the ground.

This graceful horse, with its Thoroughbred, Morgan and Narragansett Pacer blood, makes a splendid riding horse with plenty of character and spirit. It stands at 15 to 16 hands and is most often gray, chestnut, black or gray, with roan, golden or palomino being rarer.

The Morgan   Just one founding stallion, foaled in 1793, was responsible for today's breed. Figure, the stallion, came to be known as Justin

Morgan after his owner. Believed to be almost pure Welsh Cob, Morgan may have had Thoroughbred blood as well. Of great character and stamina, Morgan was remarkably versatile as a farm horse, in harness and in weightpulling and racing contests – which he never lost. This extraordinary horse was also a prolific breeder and his offspring were united in their similarity of appearance and temperament. Height of the Morgan horse varies from 14 to over 15 hands and it can be bay, brown, black or chestnut. Its good-tempered and thrifty nature has made it a popular harness and riding horse.

The Tennessee Walking Horse   Like the Saddlebred, the Tennessee Walker is distinguished by an unusual and unique gait – that of a gliding, running walk that cannot be taught to any other breed. It is now practically hereditary in the Tennessee Walking Horse, which was bred from a Standard bred trotter (with Morgan and Hambletonian ancestry) at the end of the last century. The breed also

has Thoroughbred, Saddlebred and Narragansett Pacer blood. They stand at 15 – 16 hands and any solid color occurs.

The Palomino   Regarded in the United States as a breed, the Palomino is undeniably a striking horse with its golden coat and near-white mane and tail. It is believed to be of Spanish descent and is also known as the Isabella after Queen Isabella, who promoted the breed in the fifteenth century. The palomino color is seen in the Quarter Horse, Morgan and Saddlebred.

Eastern Europe
Poland has a dedicated horse-breeding program, notably in the development of the ancient tarpan (described in Chapters 1 and 2) and with its own breeds, the dun Konik pony, the dun Hucul pony, the chestnut Sokolsky farmhorse, the Wielkopolski and the Malapolski. Poland's interest in breeding is perhaps indicated by the huge horse population of some three million.

The Wielkopolski   Of many different foreign bloods, this lean,

Allah said to the South Wind: "Become solid flesh, for I will make a new creature of thee, to the honor of My Holy One, and the abasement of Mine enemies, and for a servant to them that are subject to Me."
And the South Wind said: "Lord, do Thou so".
Then Allah took a handful of the South Wind and he breathed thereon, creating the horse and saying: "Thy name shall be Arabian, and virtue bound into the hair of thy forelock, and plunder on thy back. I have preferred thee above all beasts of burden, inasmuch as I have made thy master thy friend. I have given thee the power of flight without wings, be it in onslaught or in retreat, I will set men on thy back, that shall honor and praise Me and sing Hallelujah to My name."

Bedouin legend

Below and center: **The Arab has been exported all over the world, particularly since the sixteenth century. The English** Thoroughbred is just one breed to have developed from Arab blood, and many others have benefited from the introduction of Arab stallions – exceptionally graceful and powerful animals.

powerfully built horse is popular both as a riding and driving horse, while the heavier types are good farmworkers. They stand between 15.2 and 16.2 hands and are usually brown.

The Malapolski Native tarpan-type Polish stock was crossed with Arabians to produce a longlegged lightweight riding horse. Sound, with plenty of stamina and an easy action, the Malapolski is exported to various countries. Its height can be up to 16 hands and any color occurs.

Yugoslavia works about 400,000 of its Bosnian ponies, descended from the tarpan and the Arab. Czechoslovakia boasts the Kladruber breed

dating from the late 1570s. It is Hungary, however, that shows an interest in horse-breeding comparable to Poland's, with its draft horse, the Murakoser, the elegant 16-hand chestnut Gidran, the 15-hand gray all-purpose Shagya Arab, and the best known, the Nonius and the Furioso, the latter descended from Nonius stock in the mid-nineteenth century.

The Nonius Founded in 1785, the stud was based on an Anglo–Norman stallion, Nonius, with Thoroughbred blood to which were sent numerous different mares, including Arab, Lipizzaner, Spanish, Turkish and native Hungarian. Selective breeding ensured consistency of the strain, and today these horses – and the Furioso as well – are extrememly popular for all sorts of horsemanship from dressage, eventing and cross-country to jumping, steeplechasing and hunting.

Soviet Union

Some 40 breeds are to be found on this huge land-mass, with its greatly varying environmental and climatic conditions. Every type of horse is represented, from the ancient indigenous breeds, still vital in vast numbers for farm work, to the riding horses bred for all sorts of competitive events and for pleasure. Heavy draft breeds include the *Russian Heavy Draft Horse, Soviet Heavy Draft Horse*, and the *Lithuanian Heavy Draft Horse*. Horsebreeding is subject to governmental control and as the program concentrates on upgrading each breed for its required purpose much foreign blood has been introduced in the past two to three hundred years. Each region of the Union is obligated to produce at least a couple of breeds. It is invidious, therefore, to select just one or two, but, certainly, the *Akhal Teké*, the *Budyonny*, the *Tersk*, the *Ukrainian* and the *Latvian* are riding horses

that should not be overlooked, while the *Orlov Trotter* and the Russian Trotter – a cross between the Orlov and the American Standardbred – compete in trotting races both at home and abroad.

Australia

Australia has bred horses only in the last 150 years or so, but its stock of feral brumbies is now supplemented with the Waler from New South Wales, its descendants the Australian Stock Horse and the Australian Pony.

Above: The Criollos of South America are bred for their hardiness. This has developed as a consequence of their fight for survival on poorly vegetated plains.

Cowboys rounding up the North American mustangs. The Broncos, the most devilish of the strain, are bred for rodeo appearances, at which they display their spectacular dislike of the rider.

Overleaf: **Half-wild horses in Hungary. They provided the basic stock – together with Arab and English horses – for many Hungarian breeds.**

Riding Games—

Speed and Courage

The horse in history was required principally for war and for work, but as long ago as 1,000 BC the horse featured in games and sports. Chariot racing was popular with the ancient Greeks. They included it as an event in the Olympic Games when they established them at Olympia in 776 BC, in honor of Zeus, the supreme god.

Ancient games and sports are sometimes difficult to differentiate from hunting. Games naturally reflected the fact that man's survival depended on finding food. Pig-sticking, lionhunting and falconry began through the need to kill wild animals for food, and have consequently become outmoded. Sports, such as bullfighting and polo, have survived to this day as demonstrations of the skill and rapport of horse and rider. Their interest has not diminished. During the Age of Chivalry, jousting tournaments enjoyed a great popularity with the medieval knights who could demonstrate their prowess without enduring the discomfort of the battlefield. These tournaments were somewhat frowned upon by the Church because they constituted a form of adultery which was sanctioned by the aristocracy. Each knight would select a desirable woman – preferably married to someone of higher rank – who would reward him in the appropriate manner if he proved himself worthy during the day's jousting spectacle.

The knights used blunted lances, but the sport was nevertheless dangerous and required considerable skill and horsemanship if wounds, inflicted at the gallop, were to be avoided. The tournaments were a costly exercise too, because the knight would be expected to deck himself out in full armor and provide livery for his servants and sumptuous decoration for his horse.

It was consequently considered outrageous if the lady of his choice withheld her favours – tired and bloody though the knight might be. As the Age of Chivalry progressed, medieval tournaments became more and more of a spectacle – with the continuing disapproval of the Church – and although steps were taken to make them safer, vicious conflicts were not uncommon.

Medieval jousting can still be seen in some parts of Europe, notably England, but these have mostly become innocuous affairs forming a part of festivals. Showmanship and the visible expertise of horse and rider however has by no means died out. An ancient example is the game of buzhaski which still survives today in Afghanistan.

Buzhaski

In common with pigsticking, lion-hunting and falconry, buzhaski is a

These pages: **The ancient game of buzhaski still played in northern Afghanistan is essentially a complex tug-of-war that requires immense skill.**

game that has its origins in the quest for food. It is essentially, according to tradition, a tug-of-war over a goat – nowadays, however, a newly killed calf is normally used. The game has been played in various parts of Asia, under the name of buzhaski, kok buri or baiga. Considerable ceremony attends the contest with the horses – which have been on a nutritious diet for weeks in advance – decked out in velvet saddlecloths embroidered in gold and silver.

The goat or calf is picked up by the fastest rider, who has to swoop to the ground while controlling his galloping steed. The goal is to gallop up to a post just over a mile (2 km) away go round it and back to where he originally picked up the animal. The skill lies in keeping hold of the calf while controlling the horse and, at the same time, warding off the other riders who will be attempting to wrest it from

his grasp. Since all the riders are galloping at full pelt, each leaning this way and that, it takes acute timing and agility to stay astride, avoiding the melee of flashing hooves, let alone keeping hold of the calf.

The real excitement comes when two riders are racing neck and neck with each other, the one leaning over and trying to capture the prize from the other.

The lead rider is unlikely to reach his goal unchallenged: thunderous hooves sound behind him, mixing with the crack of whips. The competitors flail each other with the whips and this is just an added deterrent in the formidable process of recovering the animal once it has slipped from the grasp of the lead rider.

Buzhaski is played on the huge, infertile areas of the steppes by landowners and peasants alike, regardless of age. It is a game in

which years of experience have more to contribute than energy, and the accomplished contestants are likely to be 40 years old or more. Buzhaski demands courage and tenacity and a certain recklessness. These are the qualities that make the professional players, the Chupandos. They are normally retained by a landowner who provides them with a horse that has been bred and trained specifically for the purpose.

The horses used are usually the Turkoman light horse, known variously in the past as the Bactrian,

Above: **Often thirty or forty men tussle for the dead animal's body.**

the Turanian, and the Turk. It is descended from the Mongolian wild horse and it is now bred in neighboring Iran. The breed stands at about 15.2 hands and can be any solid color. It shows particular aptitude for racing over long distances, being very fast and strong with excellent endurance. Nomadic tribesmen of Asia have long kept the smaller horses (about 14 – 15 hands), probably chiefly for use with livestock. They have also been the principal stock of various cavalries in the East, and their speed now makes them a coveted racehorse in Iran, as well as a valuable asset to the daring buzhaski player.

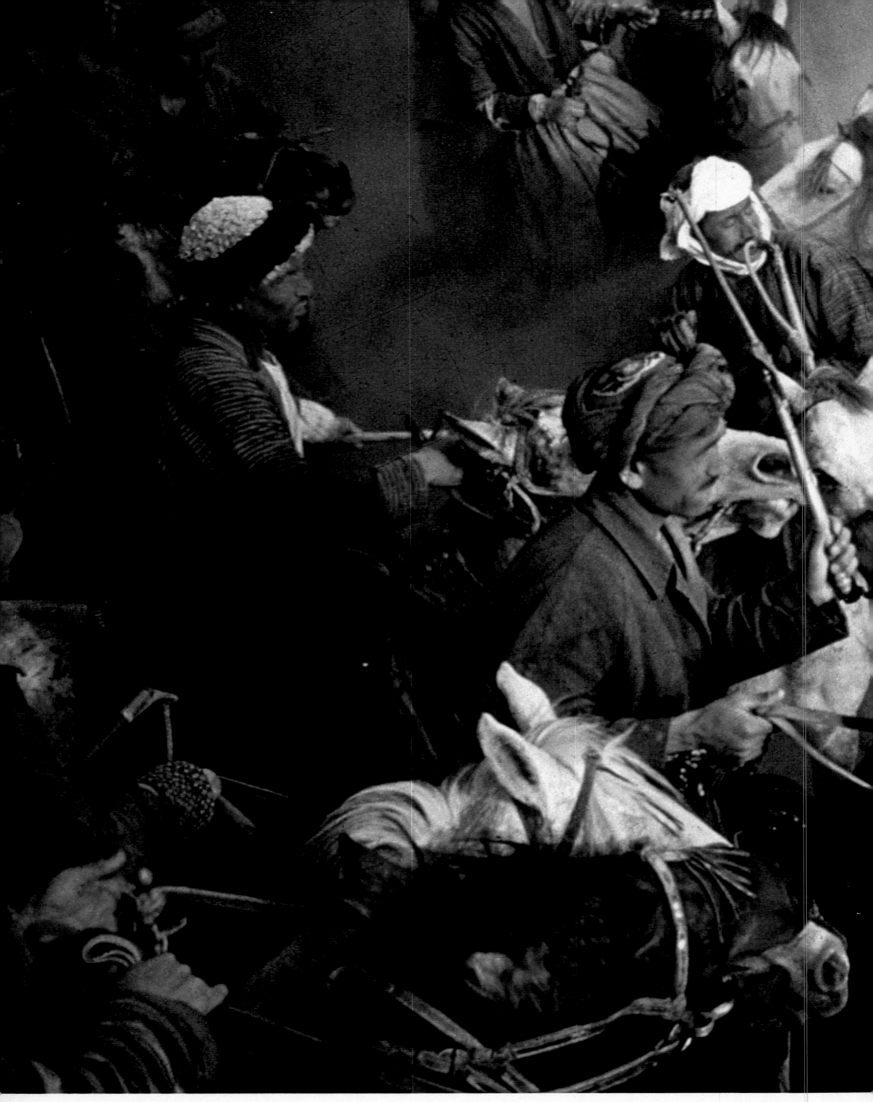

The buzhaski horses have to be tremendously agile, quick and fearless as the riders vie with each other to capture the prize of a newly killed goat or calf.

These pages: **The Chupandos, the buzhaski competitors, value their horses above anything else and regardless of** **the excitement of the game make sure their horses are kept warm at the end.**

Pigsticking

The gruesome, centuries old game of pigsticking – the hunt for the boar – may be compared with bullfighting in terms of its ferocity and danger. There the comparison stops, however, for bullfighting is essentially a spectator sport with little or no connection with the hunt for food, while pigsticking was intended for the sportsman's amusement and for his table.

The boar is one of the fiercest and fastest of all wild animals. He can weigh some 340 lb (150 kg) and for the first half mile can run as fast as a horse. The boar is an awesome target, for, like the bull, he is horned and it is said that these razor sharp devices can disembowel a man or a horse.

Pigsticking dates to the ancient civilizations of Greece, Rome and Persia, when men hunted the boar on foot with the spear. By the Middle Ages, pigsticking on horseback was common in Europe and the British introduced it to India in the eighteenth century.

Man and mount would track the boar and, as it charged, the rider would throw his spear. Great agility was required, for if the spear missed the oncoming boar horse and rider would have to beat a hasty retreat. If the spear failed to penetrate a fatal spot, the wounded boar was likely to continue the charge and fight, resulting in a bloody engagement. The sport saw some regulation in the eighteenth century when the hunters divided themselves into heats with only one heat allowed to chase the boar at any one time. As soon as he was spotted, the leader of the closest heat would take his team into the chase in an arrow–shape formation, so that when the boar attempted to veer off first in one direction and then in another, he could be speared from a number of angles.

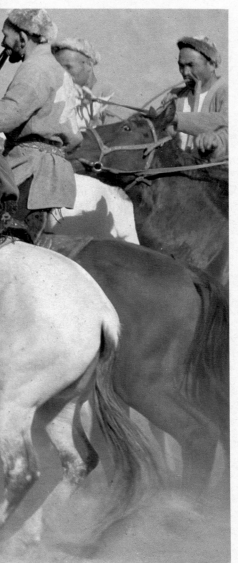

Other such sports in past centuries include elephant hunting, lion hunting and giraffe hunting practised by the white man in Africa. The giraffe's only means of defence was the speed of his escape but the elephant and lion often proved a lot more daunting. Sudanese tribes, mounted on horses descended from Barbs, used to hunt elephants as well, by first provoking it to charge, and then galloping away while other tribesmen came up from the rear to kill the animal with swords and spears.

Sports today

Many equestrian sports and activities today are rooted in a basic need such as the hunt for food or some other reflection of a past way of life. Once a traditional way of life has passed or become less widespread, those with the requisite skills for it have been reluctant to let them die. This is evident especially in the popularity of the American rodeo, at which the traditional skills of the ranchers are displayed for the crowd.

With the increased mechanization of the twentieth century, on the one hand the need for horses was greatly reduced and, on the other, much more leisure time became available. Polo, bullfighting, hunting, showjumping, dressage, eventing, racing and harness racing are all competitive equestrian

Above and overleaf: **Years of practice count for more than the energy of youth in this ferocious game.**

225

Below: **The oldest team game in the world, the one-time game of khans and caliphs, moguls and maharajahs is, however, not only a question** of money, status and background: **polo is a game for tough men who also have to be first-class riders.**

activities with long histories, that are as popular in the twentieth century as they have ever been.

Polo

The game of polo takes its name from the Tibetan word for ball, *pulu*, Tibet being one of the countries where polo was first played. Polo is probably the fastest team game in the world with a devoted and enthusiastic following. It was included as part of the Olympic Games at various times in the first 30 years of this century. Nowadays, it is Argentina who has achieved prominence in the game with most of Europe's mounts being bred there and Argentina producing three times as many polo players as any other country.

Polo has been played in various different forms in Asia for the past 2,000 years, notably in Persia, Tibet and Mongolia. The game has always been regarded as the pleasure of the aristocracy and it was a great favorite in the 400 years of the Moghul empire. This great empire, with its artistic and cultural achievements, spread from Mongolia to invade India where it founded an empire in 1526.

Persian manuscripts and Chinese watercolors testify to the popularity of the game elsewhere in Asia. A traveller to Persia in the early seventeenth century noted that "The King of Persia and his nobles take exercise by playing pall-mall on horseback…; their horses are so well trained to this that they run after the ball like cats."

The game spread to Europe from India through the British tea planters and army officers, who discovered the game in the 1850s. The team spirit, discipline and the fighting element of the game all had a natural appeal, and when those army officers returned to England they took the game with them.

The game is played by two teams of four men – two forwards, a halfback and a back – with mallets which have long, flexible handles. The idea is to drive the ball down the field and through the goalposts. The game is normally played under handicap from 0 to 10, the team's handicap being calculated by the sum of its members' handicaps. A match comprises four or six chukkas, each of 7 ½ minutes, with intervals in which the ponies are changed. A pony rarely plays more than two chukkas since the speed of the game, the swinging and fast turns, are considered too exhausting.

The game starts with the halfback or center half initiating the attack on the opposing team's goal. He has to hit long and hard and, as the forwards take up the ball, defend from the rear. As the forwards gallop into action they have to get the ball into goal, avoiding a skirmish with the opposing forwards. Stringent rules apply to polo in order to reduce the possibility of accidents. A player must not ride right across an opponent at full gallop, nor must he zigzag or jostle. Even in the full excitement of the game each player must remember not to hook unless the ball is between him and his opponent, nor must he pass the mallet between the horse's legs, over the croup or under its neck.

Important matches use three umpires to ensure fair play – and if the rules are overlooked in the single-minded pursuit of the ball, then a player may be sent off and a free hit awarded to the opposing team. Two of the three umpires follow the game on the field and a third is positioned on the touchline to act as referee in the event of dispute.

This immensely fast game requires, ideally, a horse with perfect balance, a light mouth and the ability to go straight into the gallop. Above all, it needs to be responsive, very agile, fast and calm. The player needs a good eye and anticipation, with a positive gift for timing – and all this

Above: **Patient training and a skilled rider are required to control the polo pony, whose instinct will be to** **follow the others rather than surge forward to win.**

on a horse that can turn on a dime. Stirrups are often shortened to allow the player maximum mobility without losing his seat. The great American player, Milton Devereux, said that the horse is a good 60 per cent of any man's game.

The horses are always referred to as polo ponies, and this was accurate in the nineteenth century, when the supreme polo pony was the Manipur at 11 – 13 hands. The English tea planters rode Manipur ponies, which were said to be quick, surefooted and alert. The Burma or Shan pony, at about 13 hands, was used by British officers in Burma, but this was probably less than the ideal mount. South Africa's Basuto pony, at 14.2 hands, was an enduring favourite, however, with its fearlessness and terrific stamina.

Below: **Both horse and rider wear protective devices as they play polo – a fast and potentially dangerous game.**

Today's polo pony, however, is not strictly speaking, a pony, as it stands at about 15 hands and most of the world's polo ponies now have Thoroughbred blood. The polo pony can be culled from any breed; what is demanded is a good, long neck, sturdy shoulders, a short back, powerful, sloping hindquarters on well letdown hocks. The game has no place for the timid pony, so a certain liveliness and courage are sought in the ideal mount.

The Argentinians took their native Criollo and crossed it with the Thoroughbred to start what is now a thriving horsebreeding industry. Thoroughbred stock has been

Above: **Polo ponies' tails are bandaged before the game to prevent their entanglement.**

introduced repeatedly in a country which displaced even the United States' supremacy at the game in the first 40 years of this century. Today, Argentina is recognized as the world's foremost polo playing nation. Whereas in Europe the game has been dominated by the aristocracy – and it certainly is an expensive game – in Argentina the rich, the landowners and the cattle workers alike all take part.

Because in important matches ponies complete no more than two chukkas and there are four or six chukkas to a match, each player has to have several ponies at his disposal and this accounts in part for the expense of the game. Additionally, the ponies have to be rigorously trained for a long period of time to bring them up to the required standard. Even then, it is the player's natural eye for the ball, his skill, experience of the game and his handling of his mount that is crucial.

Some controversy exists over whether pure horsemanship is the key or whether it is the natural instinct of the ballplayer that is paramount. Charles Chevenix Trench, noted horsemen and historian, has written that "A good polo-player must, of course, be a reasonably good rider, but there are some firstclass polo-players who are not firstclass horsemen, and some firstclass horsemen who are indifferent polo-players. It is more important to have the eye and aggressive instinct of a game-player, to be able to hit the ball hard and accurately and, above all, to have the gift of anticipation, to estimate in an instant where the ball and other players are going next, and to place oneself accordingly. The man without this essential game sense, however good a horseman, will too often find himself galloping madly in the wrong direction."

"Seventy girls rode out onto the field in fervent ardor before their queen. In courage each one was like the Isfandiar, in their skill with the bow they were equal to the knights and they played polo so well that they played as when the sun rises and a falcon swoops down to catch a partridge."
Nisami, Persian writer (1140 – 1202).

Overleaf: **The speed of the game defies even the camera. The riders wear helmets, for even if they fall, the game goes on and injury is hard to avoid.**

Bullfighting

Fighting the bull was an ancient sport, but in its present form may be traced back to the Dark Ages, developing in European countries from hunting on open country. Certainly, by the eleventh century it had become a popular spectator sport. Often extremely dangerous for bull, horse and rider, the sport was so enjoyed by the sixteenth century that the Pope felt compelled to ban it in 1558. Classical equitation as exemplified today by the Spanish Riding School in Vienna was highly favored in Spain at this time. Andalusian horses were trained to the highest degree of perfection, allowing them to excel at the *rejoneo*, or bullfight. The Spanish adopted the savage

practices of horse training used by the Neapolitans in the seventeenth century, and today the toothed noseband, the *cerreta*, is still used to control the horse. The bull was to be killed with the *rejon*, the spear, by the *rejoneador* from the back of his horse or, alternatively, wounded or killed with a spike, the *garrocha*, hurled while still mounted. The contestant would then dismount if necessary to complete the kill with the *rejon*.

Mounted bullfighting in accordance with tradition survives in Portugal and in some parts of Spain. In most parts of Spain, however, the bull is fought from the ground. This is partly the result of the influence of

Above: Complete rapport between rider and horse is essential in the bullfighting ring if danger is to be avoided.

King Philip of Anjou who, in the seventeenth century, turned the sport from one of the aristocracy to one of the people. He considered bullfighting a dangerous, dirty business, and, as a Frenchman, infinitely preferred more courtly pastimes.

Considerable ceremony attends the bullfight in Spain and in Portugal, with toreadors or rejoneadors often clad in silver or white. Their mounts are dearly prized, often Andalusians which will have been schooled in *haute école*:

"The art of *rejoneo* obliges the horse trained in the Andalusian manner, when facing the bull in the arena, to execute all figures – *suertes* – up to the decisive stab – *rejon* .... needless to dwell on the training, submissiveness and obedience, let alone suppleness, required of these horses ..."

Once considered the most noble horse in Europe, the Andalusian has been crossed with Thoroughbred and Arab to produce a horse with the desired characteristics of good stamina, courage, spirit and intelligence. The horses are trained tirelessly, for the rejoneador knows that to tangle with an enraged bull can only mean disaster, if not death. The *cerreta*, or spiked noseband, is used so that the horse's mouth remains sensitive. His long training in paces and movements culminates in confrontation with an extraordinary contraption consisting of a pair of horns mounted on a bicycle wheel. A small boy propels the bicycle this way and that in imitation of an angry bull. As the horse learns the commands and perfects his movements, he is gradually promoted to practicing with a tame bull until he is considered ready for the ring. The bulls are bred specially for speed and ferocity in the arena. They are tested on the Spanish plains, where they are reared, by *vaqueros* (cowboys).

A somewhat happier fate awaits the Portuguese bull than the Spanish: in Spain the goal is to kill the beast, while in Portugal this is frowned upon. The Portuguese believe that the display should be entirely a spectacle of unparalleled horsemanship, deftly avoiding bull with a turn and a pirouette. The Portuguese bullfighter has only to sink a dart in the bull's hindquarters to claim the contest.

Above: **At the start of the contest, the rejoneador and the horse adopt a challenging stance to await the charge of** **the bull. Within seconds, they will display their skill as they evade the thrust of the horns.**

Previous page: **For centuries the pleasure of the aristocracy, foxhunting is now practiced by the gentry and** local farmers and riders alike. **The hounds – querulous and alert – search out the scent of the fox.**

Hunting on Horseback

Foxhunting

Animals such as lion, gazelle, boar, elephant and stag have all been hunted for centuries but the peculiarly English art of foxhunting is more related to the thrill of the chase than to the capture of the prey. Many dukes and earls kept their own packs of hounds in medieval times and they hunted the fox over huge, open tracts of land. As the land was gradually subjected to enclosure – a process that started in the twelfth century and continued through to the nineteenth – so the practice of jumping the fences and ditches started, naturally increasing the risk and excitement of the hunt. The newly moneyed classes of the early nineteenth century increased the popularity of the sport to a point where subscription packs of hounds became common, with a Master appointed by a committee. Foxes became scarce in some areas, and so the practice began of introducing them specially for the hunt. This disgraceful practice was outlawed at the end of the nineteenth century with strict rules enforced by the newly formed Master of Foxhounds Association. Foxhunting is a sport beloved of the English and Irish – and, by the end of the nineteenth century, by Americans, notably in Virginia. The style of riding favored for the hunt was the open gallop on a free rein. This was frowned upon in Europe, where classic horsemanship – at its zenith in the style of the Spanish Riding School – was still thought to be the peak of equestrian achievement.

Stamina and fearless jumping are the most desirable characteristics of the hunter, as well as agility and responsiveness. Hunters often have Thoroughbred blood, or may be pure Thoroughbred.

These pages: **Foxhunting has lost none of the ceremony of centuries past and even today Master of the Hounds calls to his pack with the horn.**

The Lipizzaners of the Spanish Riding School of Vienna perform astonishing spectacles –
here one of the stallions executes the ballotade with an arrow-straight back and legs tucked
well into the body.

The Spanish Riding School

school-horse, hunter or charger, and the methods employed by this famous riding-master have been preserved at the Spanish Riding School."

The three-year training is carried out in three one-year phases: the first in which horse and rider are schooled in "riding straight forward" at the normal paces, maintaining a supple and natural carriage and seat; the second in which the rider is taught to control the horse with a greater degree of collection, with care in maintaining the pace and the suppleness, and to master more unusual paces. Pupils are taught how to effect a rapid change of the leading leg while cantering, and they are also instructed in gaits and turns which include the pirouette, the passade, the passage, and the piaffe.

The third phase concentrates on high school equitation(*haute école*) and the demanding maneuvers known as airs above the ground – the *capriole*, the *ballotade* and the *croupade*.

The *capriole* requires the horse to leap in the air, the rider remaining quite vertical and straightbacked, with its forelegs tucked under the body and hindlegs outstretched completely straight behind him. The *ballotade* and the *croupade* are, again, leaps, but this time both the forelegs and the hindlegs must be tucked into the body. The *croupade* must see the horse tucking its legs under its belly so that the shoes cannot be seen. The *ballotade* require the hindlegs to be tucked tighter into the body, but the horse's shoes are visible.

All the stages of training in the Spanish School include many different and very complex maneuvers with several variations of each movement. To excel in this style of riding was, and still is by some, considered to be the accomplishment of supreme elegance and control in riding. Critics of the style protest, however, that it has little relevance to hunting and crosscountry training skills and, in addition, subjects the horse to outmoded, uncomfortable movements. The style never achieved particular popularity in Great Britain, where riders have traditionally preferred the greater thrills and dash of foxhunting, racing and steeplechasing.

From the time that Xenophon (c. 430 – c. 355 BC), the great Greek general, historian and writer, published his work on horsemanship, the advocates of the various European styles have hotly disputed the ideal. Only in the twentieth century was there a complete revolution in riding style, wrought by the Italian Federico Caprilli who advocated the forward seat in jumping and eventing, with an emphasis on the horse's freedom to move naturally. In the art of dressage, however, the Spanish Riding School of Vienna is still believed by many to be the supreme achievement in control and discipline of the horse.

The Renaissance courts of Europe produced three chief styles of classical equitation and these were the Spanish School of Vienna, the Portuguese of Marialva and the French, first at Versailles and then at Saumur. The Spanish and Portuguese favored a high degree of collection and control, while the French approved a lighter, high-stepping, more showy style. At the same time, the Swedish and German styles were followed in those countries with their greater emphasis on discipline, rein control and leg aids, their proponents considering that the horse above all must be obedient and that innate intelligence could not be assumed. All these styles existed chiefly for teaching cavalry officers to ride – none more so than the Spanish School of Vienna, which was established by 1572. Andalusians were considered at that time to be the most desirable breed in Europe, and so it was the Spanish horses and the Spanish style of riding that were offered to the Austrian cavalry.

In 1751, François Robichon de la Guerinière published his École de Cavalerie, quickly to become the Bible of the Spanish School, and a text which today is no less valid in its description of the three-year training. Nearly 200 years later Alois Podhajsky, director of the School from 1939 to 1965, wrote that Guerinière's intention was "to obtain by systematic work a riding-horse that was quiet, supple and obedient, pleasant in his movements and comfortable for his rider. These are the requirements for any

– Riding to Perfection

"The horse can never be made to perfect the form in which it expresses its ability by force, but only by a carefully harmonized interplay between flattering and demanding, between much praise and little punishment."
Alois Podhajsky,
Spanish Riding School,
Vienna

These pages: **The Spanish Riding School of Vienna was founded to teach not only classic equestrianism to the highest standard but to verse** its riders in feats such as the **levade (top) and the capriole.**

Overleaf: **The traditional transport of Hungarian mail is still preserved to provide a spectacle and an example of expert horsemanship.**

Hans Günter Winkler

The most successful show
jumper in the world: won
seven Olympic medals –
including five golds – and
two world championships.

I have always been mad about horses. Of all the horses that I have been fortunate enough to ride, there is one that still stands out from all the others in my mind after all these years – the mare Halla. A horse that a rider comes across only once in a lifetime. This mare, about which so much has been written and reported, was an exception in every way: we – both of us had been brought together quite by chance – were united for over a decade by a common bond which can only be described, without exaggeration, as a great love, although there had been some trouble at first. Halla, who had an unusually strong personality and was not to be trifled with, had considerable difficulty in adapting to me in the beginning. Much effort was needed in conjunction with great patience to bring this wilful prima donna under control. But as the mare was extremely intelligent, she allowed herself to be persuaded by my apparently more convincing arguments. The result was that this unmanageable lady became a partner I could rely on in every way in tricky situations.

Our first great test came in the 1953 World Championship in Madrid. Here Halla and I were absolute out-siders in this great international event.

After we had qualified for the final among the last four, which in itself was quite surprising in the situation at that time, the last battle began. After all these years, I can still see the very beautiful arena in the Club de Campo in Madrid as if it had all happened only yesterday. There was not one empty seat left in the riding stadium, which had been specially built for this world championship. Everyone who was anyone was there to see the great favorite, Paco Goyaga, their own countryman, win. At first it looked very much as if that was what was going to happen, since when the horse was changed, which is usual in world championship finals, everything seemed to favor Paco. But I, too, was only just behind the favorite by one jumping error as the result of a few lucky rounds. Then – in the next to last round – something happened which made me and the tens of thousands in the stand hold our breath. Major Garcia Cruz, the second Spanish competitor in the finals, was riding Halla. The very first jumps clearly showed that there was a disharmony between rider and horse, which could only be made up for by the tremendous jumping ability of my mare. But the best will on the part of Halla was of no avail. Through the extra help from the rider she jumped off too soon at a large oxer and landed in the middle of this very solid monster. The result was a bad knock, although the mare's skill kept her on her legs, followed by a cry from the crowd. Halla was standing on three legs in the middle of the arena and holding her right foreleg up in front of her. I ran to see what had happened. The finals were interrupted to allow Halla to be attended by a vet. Thank heavens that a careful examination showed that the heavy impact on the obstacle had "only" bruised a nerve and that the mare could be ridden again after brief treatment.

Any other horse would hardly have shown the same outstanding performance after such a shock. But Halla did. In the last round she carried me to my first win in a show-jumping world championship which would be the beginning of a great and wonderful series of successes in the life of Halla and me.

Hans Günter Winkler

Showjumping —

Spills and Thrills

Showjumping

Showjumping is the most spectacular of equestrian sports. In recent years, largely through television, it has become hugely successful with the public. Speed, daring, and precision create a suspense that keeps spectators on the edge of their seats. Great demands are made on both horse and rider in today's highly competitive and potentially lucrative world of showjumping. It is, however, a comparatively recent horse sport. Jumping as a sport developed primarily out of foxhunting – hence the traditional red coats of many riders. During the second half of the nineteenth century, skill in jumping began to be tested separately. The Royal Dublin Society Horse Show in 1868 included a competition for the "high leap" and the "wide leap". In 1883, Madison Square Gardens in New York hosted the first US National Horse Show, which

This page: **Top riders have their own styles though they can be much influenced by national training and tradition. Seen here are: the Austrian** Hugo Simon (left), the West German Alwin Schockemöhle (right) and Gert Wiltfang (top).

Below: **The West German Fritz Ligges won Olympic gold medals as individual champion in 1964 and as a team member in 1972.**

included jumping competitions. In 1900, jumping competitions were first included in the Olympic Games.

From these beginnings, jumping as a test of the horse's schooling, performance and the rider's skill soon assumed a prominence and interest that was to bring show-jumping to the forefront of inter-national equestrian sports. School-ing was, and still is, the keynote to the success of a showjumper. This may account for the prominence of West German showjumpers, as the Germans emphasize a high degree of schooling and dressage.

From its beginnings, just 100 years ago, showjumping has now become one of the world's four chief equestrian sports, together with eventing, dressage and combined driving.

Because showjumping developed in the United States and European countries in parallel – to be followed by Australia – there was a consequent diversity, not only of rules and but also organization of events. There were also differences in the styles of riding and techniques of encouraging a horse

Above: **Major Paul Weier has been the Swiss champion for nearly 20 years. He has competed in the Olympics since 1960 and in the Men's European Championships.**

Overleaf: **The Italian rider, Raimondo D'Inzeo, was World Champion in 1956 and 1960. He has also won gold and silver medals in Olympic competitions.**

253

to clear a jump, as well as in the design of courses and the jumps themselves.

International styles

Up until the end of the nineteenth century, classical horsemanship, as epitomized today by the Spanish Riding School of Vienna, was considered in Europe to be the correct way to ride. Cavalry officers in particular strove to achieve the highly disciplined style that resulted from a great degree of collection by use of the aids. Aids are, essentially, the rider's control of the horse by the hands through the reins, to the bit which, through its contact with the horse's mouth, controls its speed and direction; the legs, pressure and position of which guide the horse and also control speed; the weight through the rider's seat, and the distribution of the rider's weight in relation to the horse's center of gravity; the voice for commands; and, to a lesser extent, the whip and spurs.

At the end of the nineteenth century, riders tended to favor an upright or even backward seat with stirrup leathers so long that their legs were almost straight. Even when jumping, it was felt that if the rider leaned back while the horse jumped, it would somehow counteract the horse's changing center of gravity and "help" it over the jump.

The Italian, Federico Caprilli (1868 – 1907), changed all this with his promotion of the "forward" seat. Caprilli pointed out that the horse would be "helped" over a jump in particular if the rider leaned forward so that there would be no backward drag.

English riders had taken no great interest in classical horsemanship anyway, much preferring the rough and tumble of the hunting-field. America and Australia were too isolated geographically to be greatly influenced much by the niceties of European horsemanship. At about the time that Caprilli was causing a furore in Europe with his revolutionary methods, American jockeys visited Europe: their startling forward seat with short stirrup leathers lent support to Caprilli's claims.

The significance of shorter stirrup leathers lies in the fact that they allow the rider to stand up and lean forward over the horse's neck as it jumps, thus giving the horse maximum freedom to clear the obstacle.

The early years of the twentieth century saw an increasing interest in showjumping. The International Horse Show at Olympia in 1907 held jumping competitions.

The Show had been organized and largely financed by Americans but its original planning, two years before, took place in Holland. For this reason it was announced that: "the numerous jumps are closer together than is usual at British shows, and a judge at each jump jots down the points earned by each horse, the highest total number of points obtained by any horse constituting the winner. This is the Continental system."

The winner of the first 12 jumping competitions received £ 100 in prize money – not only a substantial sum at the time but twice as much as any other showjumping prize before it.

In the last years of the nineteenth century and the first years of the twentieth, jumps – whether outdoor

Above: **Even the international rider experiences the occasional mishap.**

or indoor – largely imitated the sort of obstacle the rider would encounter in the open although they were generally very flimsy. As jumping became increasingly competitive, however, different sorts of jumps were introduced; doubles, trebles and combinations of existing jumps appeared, course design became a major consideration – and, with the sport achieving international status, the rules and organization of each event came under the control of the FEI (Fédération Equestre Internationale). The FEI was established in 1921 to initiate a standardization in showjumping rules and organization; up until that time there was considerable diversity both from show to show and from country to country.

Naturally enough, the FEI rulings on course design, types of jumps and method of judging all influenced international riding styles. Italian cavalry officers outshone practically everyone else, influenced as they were by Caprilli's teachings in the first twenty years of the century. More recently, however, it is West German riders who have excelled all over Europe as champions of the "Parcours".

The professional circuit

Those who choose to make showjumping their professional career will indeed be kept busy. The showjumping season now extends right around the calendar with both outdoor and indoor shows. For those who are successful in the numerous affiliated events there are the European, Junior European and World Championships and Olympic Games. Riders have to qualify for the championship events and of course they must be selected to represent their countries in the Olympic Games. Among the most prestigious for the showjumper are the Official Internationals (CSIOs) and Ordinary Internationals (CSIs). The cumulative successes of the riders at these events are used to select a team for the annual team championships. In addition, points gained in the CSIOs are awarded to each rider in respect of the country he or she represents. From these Nations Cups, the nation with the most points takes the President's Cup, established in 1965.

The CSIOs are held in Nice, Rome, Lisbon, Barcelona, Madrid, Geneva, Aachen, Leipzig, Rotterdam and Copenhagen, of which Aachen is said to be the most formidable. At Hickstead, England, the British Nations Cup and the British Jumping Derby are contested. The latter, with its 10'6" (3,2 meters) bank to negotiate, is even more prestigious than the Hamburg Derby, established in 1929.

Indoor and outdoor jumping competitions each have their advocates. The indoor ring requires enormous precision from the horse, which needs to be able to turn very quickly and not be upset by bright lights and an enclosed atmosphere. The outdoor event demands a horse with perhaps more dash and a longer stride.

One of the most notable of the indoor competitions is the Horse of the Year Show held each autumn at Wembley, England. In North America there is the National in New York City, the Washington International, the Pennsylvania National at Harrisburg, and the Royal Winter Fair at Toronto in

Above right: **Great riders have to start early. The colored rosette signifies victory.**

Canada. The American jumping hold international competitions and these, too, are governed by the FEI. Otherwise, equestrian events in America are controlled by the American Horse Shows Association. Australia's showjumping circuit has seen a slow standardization since the early 1950s, when FEI rules were introduced. Strict quarantine regulations prevail against foreign competitors, but Australian riders have competed in the Olympic Games since 1964 and at various overseas events including Wembley's Royal International Horse Show.

The course

Fences in showjumping courses were originally quite similar to obstacles encountered in the hunting field, but as showjumping became more popular and more competitive, with ever increasing sums of prize money at stake, so jumps became more imaginative. The design of a course is dependent on the size of the arena itself, the position of the judges, the type, number and position of fences to be accommodated and the distance between each fence, as well as the overall standard of complexity required. The distance between each fence and the angling of each obstacle is an important consideration when designing the course – there is no point, after all, in designing a course so formidable as to be impossible or one so easy that all competitors get clear rounds. There are basically two types of jumps: the upright and the spread. Many would put the water jump in a class of its own – although it is in fact a spread jump – because it presents special problems such as a horse's instinctive fear of water. Upright jumps include gates, walls, poles and the balustrade such as the one seen commonly at Hickstead. The spread jumps – which test not only the horse's ability to negotiate height but its stride and the arc of its body – include the triple bar, parallel bars and the double oxer. A true oxer is a hedge with parallel rails to back and front – and is so called because it was designed originally to prevent oxen from damaging natural hedges in the days when they were used to work the fields. Combinations of fences – doubles or trebles or even

Above left: Valuable horses need protection at all times. This horse is wearing a headguard to stop him from damaging the sensitive poll.

Above: A natural balance and tremendously powerful muscles enable jumps like these to be negotiated. Peter Luther on Livius form this competent team.

quadruples – could include, for
example, a double oxer combination over water ditches.
The level of the competition
dictates the complexity of the line
of the course, and the course
designer has to devise a line that
will test the horse's performance in
various ways.
At the international shows which
are held over several days, courses
are designed to present an
increasing difficulty each day with a
formidable grand prix to finish.
Height and width of spread fences
will vary according to the type of
fence and the competition.
Most showjumping competitions,
at least at international level, will be
set against the clock in the final
rounds, although a clear round will
beat a faster round with jumping
faults. In puissance competitions,
speed is never the important factor:
if two horses manage to jump the
same top height they will share the
winning place.

The showjumper
Powerful hindquarters are what
gives the showjumper its impulsion
and forward spring enabling it to
clear a jump. Size, breed or height
are all immaterial: it is the horse's
conformation that is crucial. The
hindquarters are the "powerhouse"
of a horse.
The body of the showjumper
should be compact, with the neck
being an important factor in the
horse's natural balance. It should be
muscular and neither too long nor
too short. Neck and shoulders
should be sloping rather than
upright with a defined arch to the
neck. Correct conformation of the
neck helps to give easier breathing
when the horse is at full stretch
over a jump. The shoulder should
not be too thick or upright, for this
is often the sign of the sturdier
horse that may not be capable of
the sort of speed needed in today's
top class showjumper. A fairly short
back is generally thought desirable
as it offers the least resistance to the
horse's impulsion, but long-backed
showjumpers have nevertheless
achieved notable success.
The legs should be strong and clean
with firm joints and tendons and
gently sloping pasterns. Very long
legs, particularly from the knee to
the pastern are not a desirable
feature of the showjumper as this

Below: **Germany's foremost
coursebuilder, Hans-Heinrich
Brinkmann, with Alwin
Schockemöhle.**

Above: **One of the world's
most gifted showjumpers,
Great Britain's David Broome,
has presented tough competition on the international
circuit for the past 25 years.**

259

Indoor horse shows, such as this one at Dortmund, West Germany, gain perhaps in popular appeal over the outdoor events. The indoor arena calls for greater precision from horse and rider and provides the spectator with a superb view.

increases the area susceptible to strain. The feet should be on the large side, so that there is a greater area to support the horse's weight as he lands after a jump.

A good jumping action is of course vital, particularly if rider or owner wants to compete internationally. The horse's head and neck should be well outstretched as he goes over a jump with the forelegs tucked up into the body and the hocks bending sharply to the ground to give him the necessary spring. He should spread out over the jump in an arc. If a horse's balance and action are good, the take off, suspension and landing will appear to be a continuous flowing movement.

Temperament is almost as important in the showjumper as build and action. If the horse is nervy and erratic, its chances of coping with the tension and the crowd at major competitions are greatly reduced. The head is the strongest indicator of temperament and, to a lesser extent, also the horse's natural balance. Key signs to an equable temperament are an intelligent, bold yet kind eye and ears that constantly prick backwards and forwards, showing alertness and awareness. A big head is not desirable, for the bigger and heavier it is, the heavier the load the horse has to lift off the ground as it jumps. Two-thirds of a horse's weight are carried in its head and forequarters.

In general, the showjumper needs to be quick, very disciplined and resilient. The ideal is the sort of temperament that positively thrives on attention and crowd response. Geldings are believed to be more stable than mares and certainly there are more of them on the international circuit. Entire horses (stallions) are rare, although they are seen.

A showjumper can theoretically be any height, but 16 hands high is about the average. Larger horses are often prone to leg trouble.

A good showjumper is worth a great deal of money, its value increasing with each successive win. As long ago as 1971, for example, West German showjumper and breeder, Paul Schockemöhle, sold Askan, his grey Hanoverian horse, for $ 100,000. International travel alone makes keeping a prize-winning showjumper an expensive business. Owner-riders today are often sponsored by large companies, or, alternatively, wealthy owners employ eminent riders to compete on their horses.

The prize money to be won in international showjumping is perhaps a reflection of the sport's increased popularity and com-

Above: **The approach and take-off are of vital importance in jumping, particularly when it comes to the huge fences of international competitions.**

Below: **Powerful hindquarters and strong, clean hocks give the showjumper the impulsion to spring forward over the jump.**

Above: **Ireland's Eddie Macken is a popular figure among competitors and spectators alike.**

petitiveness: prize money for the World Championships at Dublin in 1982 was over US $ 56,000. No one competitor could have won more than $ 18,000, however, even if he had been placed first in each of the four legs of the Championship, for each of the first three championships the winner takes one-third of the prize money, while for the final the winner takes one quarter. In the final, the four qualifying riders have to exchange horses, a telling test of any rider's ability.

Training the showjumper
No horse has an innate desire to jump but some do show a natural aptitude for it.
Even when a horse possesses a good conformation, a natural balance and an even temperament, he still has to be schooled and trained for the art of jumping. Part of such training comes under the heading of dressage.
The showjumper's initial training is no different from that of any other horse. He is gradually accustomed to the bit and the bridle and then the saddle. Using a long lunge rein, the trainer, over a period of several weeks, gets the horse used to commands as he walks and trots around in a circle. The different paces are worked at always with commands so that the horse gets used to the voice and comes to understand the various commands. After the early training on the lunge many trainers will move on to long reins. These run down from the bit and are passed through the stirrup leathers, enabling the trainer to control the horse on a sort of driving principle. All this training takes a considerable amount of time and it is vital that it is done steadily and patiently – without the horse becoming tired, confused or bored.
As schooling progresses, the trainer will teach the horse to respond to the aids (described earlier) and to changes of direction and of pace. Elementary jumping lessons may be included quite early as part of the schooling program, so that walking over poles, at least, comes naturally to the horse. After this, the horse is encouraged to trot over poles laid on the ground. From these, he progresses to cavalettis (stout wooden poles attached to a cross arrangement at either end) which

can be introduced at the end of a line of trotting poles. As the horse gets used to trotting over the poles and the cavalettis, gradually the poles can be dispensed with, and, eventually, the cavalettis raised until they resemble low jumps.
The trainer will be careful throughout any schooling program to vary the routine as much as possible. As far as jumping lessons go, this means approaching the poles and cavalettis from different angles and directions. The distance between each cavaletti will depend on the length of the horse's stride – but the length of stride can also eventually be controlled by the trainer and the rider.
Once the horse is used to jumping the raised cavalettis, small fences can be introduced – and, gradually, the horse must learn to tackle different types of fences. Small

water jumps will be introduced during schooling – these should not to be too wide in the early stages but they should not be so shallow as to encourage carelessness.
When the trainer considers the horse ready to enter for a small competition, he will take part in a preliminary or novice class. Although the course should be fairly straigthforward and the fences not too high, it will be good experience for the potential international showjumper in that it gives him the chance to get the feel of the ring and the crowd, as well as

Overleaf: **Ears pricked well forward, the horse puts all he has got into clearing this last obstacle as the sun sets.**

Below: **Hans Günter Winkler of West Germany includes among his list of successes World Championships, European Championships and Olympic gold medals.**

Below: **West Germany's Fritz Thiedemann took an individual bronze medal at the 1952 Olympics, and was in the**

West German team that won the gold medal in the 1960 Olympics.

travelling in a box. It is important that the horse is not over-faced at this point by asking him to compete in too advanced a competition.

Precision and accuracy are all important in top class show-jumping, so obedience, a good response to the aids and a fine balance are essential.

During training, the horse will have become used to varying his stride on command, this sort of control being an essential of international competitions.

When the rider walks the competition course, he will make a mental note of any sharp turns to be negotiated, the angle of approach to each fence, the type of fence and the distance between them. Accurate measurement of these distances is crucial for it is on this the rider will base his cal-culation of the horse's stride as he goes round the course.

Once in the ring, the rider has to keep many factors in mind, not least the "ground", since this will affect the horse's stride, and the horse's vision . As the horse comes up to the jump he will lower his head so that he can see the ground-line and judge the height of the fence. As he jumps, his head naturally comes up again. If the rider has the horse on too tight a rein, the horse will not be able to move his head freely and his own natural judgement will consequent-ly be impaired. Sharp turns can present a problem as well: for example, as the horse turns sharply right to come up to a fence, he can only see the fence out of his right eye as he approaches and the groundline will not be visible at all until he is able to lower his head.

Showjumping champions

West Germany

The German style of riding, with its greater attention to discipline and control, has brought West Germany great prominence in international showjumping. Gerd Wiltfang became the individual World Champion in 1978, having become a member of the West German team in 1968; from there he went on to win the King George V Gold Cup in 1971, among his many successes.

Among the great showjumpers to have emerged from Germany are the brothers Alwin and Paul Schockemöhle, Hartwig Steenken and Hans Günter Winkler. Paul Schockemöhle became European champion in 1981 and, as well as performing in the ring, he is a renowned breeder and trainer of horses. His older brother, Alwin, retired in 1976 only as a result of persistent back trouble. His successes include taking the individual gold medal at the Montreal Olympic Games (1976), having been German champion three times from 1965. Hartwig Steenken took the World Championship at Hickstead in 1974 and would clearly have pursued a brilliant career in the ring had not a fatal accident in 1977 intervened. Hans Winkler established himself as an outstanding international showjumper after 1945. He won the Olympic gold medal in 1956, and became holder of the World Championship twice and the European once. At the 1976 Olympics Hans Winkler, together with the German team, won the silver medal. He is considered one of the most successful showjumpers ever and, although now retired, continues to be active in equestrian circles.

Norbert Koof is tipped as West Germany's new young rider and was a member of the European Championship team in 1981.

Below: **Alwin Schockemöhle at the 1976 Olympic Games in Montreal where he won the individual gold medal.**

Great Britain

Whereas men appear to dominate West German showjumping, from the time of Pat Smythe's achievements in the 1950s and 1960s, Great Britain has consistently produced world class women riders. Today's household names include Caroline Bradley, Marion Mould, Jean Germany and Elizabeth Edgar – sister of David Broome. Lesley McNaught, a promising young rider under the wing of Ted Edgar, may well prove to be the Pat Smythe and Caroline Bradley of the 1980's.

Caroline Bradley is noted perhaps not so much for her spectacular successes as for her outstanding ability for getting the very best out of a horse that may not have been professionally trained from its early years. She was a team member of the winning World Championship team in 1978 at Aachen. Jean Germany is one of the new young riders in Great Britain who seems certain to become an international champion before long. She undoubtedly possesses the will to succeed.

David Broome, Harvey Smith, Eddie Macken and Malcolm Pyrah are all popular names in British and international showjumping. Harvey Smith, a colorful, controversial character, competed in the Mexico Olympic Games in 1968, but it is generally on home ground that he has been most successful. He won the British Jumping Derby at Hickstead in 1970 and 1971 and has won the John Player Trophy no less than seven times. His sons, Robert and Stephen, are set to continue the family tradition.

David Broome has had a long and dazzling career having competed in four Olympic Games, taking bronzes in 1960 and 1968. He was European champion in 1961, 1967, 1969 and in 1970 won the Men's World Championship. At home he has won the King George V Gold Cup at the Royal International Horse Show five times – an all time record – among his many successes. Eddie Macken, Ireland's outstanding showjumper, turned professional in 1975 and went into partnership with the Schockemöhle brothers in Germany. He won the British Jumping Derby in 1976, 1977 and 1978 and lost the European Championship in 1977 – by just 1/10th of a second. In the following year he came in second to Gerd Wiltfang in the World Championships.

Malcolm Pyrah has achieved more at home than abroad, but he was member of the winning World Championship team at Aachen in 1978, and in 1981 won the Aachen Grand Prix. Other outstanding British riders include Nick Skelton trained by David Broome's sister Elizabeth Edgar; Peter Robeson – Olympic competitor for over 20 years from 1956; John Whittaker; Derek Ricketts; Graham Fletcher – winner of the Aachen Grand Prix in 1975.

The United States

Although he retired after an outstanding performance in the Munich 1972 Olympics, Bill Steinkraus is still remembered as the supreme showjumping champion of America and the first American to win an Olympic gold medal for showjumping. His Olympic career started in 1952 with a bronze medal, going on to take a silver in 1960, a gold in 1968 and then leading the United States team to a silver in 1972. He won the King George V Gold Cup in 1956 and 1964.

»So the horse must be able to jump over ditches, to overcome small entrenchments and to mount heights. One should also try riding him uphill, on descending ground and downhill. For such tests show whether his spirit is courageous and his body quite sound. Many cannot do these things perhaps only because they have not practiced them, but not because they lack the energy to do so. But once they have learnt to do these things and master these exercises, they will do everything properly, as long as they are healthy and are not of bad character.«

Xenophon

These pages: **A formidable jump may unnerve the horse and dislodge the rider – showing why hard hats are essential at all times.**

America's other prominent show-jumpers have included Buddy Brown; Frank Chapot – five times Olympic competitor; Rodney Jenkins – remembered for winning US $ 125,000 on Idle Dice; Neal Shapiro – bronze medallist in the 1972 Olympic Games; Mary Chapot – the first American gold medallist at the Pan-American Games (1963); Kathy Kusner – only American woman ever to win the Women's European Championship (1967) and also an Olympic competitor; and Hugh Wiley. Today, however, it is Melanie Smith and Michael Matz, both World Cup finalists (1982 and 1981

world status in 1964 when he was beaten to an Olympic bronze medal in a jump-off with Britain's Peter Robeson. His performance through the 1960s and '70s has only recently been rivalled by Kevin Bacon and Jeff McVean.

Brazil
Of the South American countries, Argentina and Brazil in particular have competed worldwide. Brazilian Nelson Pessoa first visited Europe in 1956 and settled there in 1960, first in Switzerland and subsequently in France. He won the Men's European Championship in 1966, three Hamburg Derbies, two

enthusiastic, taking a bronze at the 1956 Olympics and becoming European champion in 1959. In 1960 he won an individual silver medal, and he helped the Italian team win bronze medals in 1960 and 1964. Piero won the King George V Gold Cup at London's International Horse Show three times.
Raimondo d'Inzeo became World Champion in 1956 and 1960, as well as distinguishing himself in the Olympics in 1956 with a silver medal, a gold in 1960, and, with his team, a bronze in 1964. He won Dublin's Grand Prix in 1975.
A gallery of the world's champion showjumpers would not be complete without mention of the German-born Hugo Simon. Not selected for the 1972 Munich Olympics, Simon obtained Austrian dual nationality through his Austrian grandmother. As an individual rider for Austria, he

respectively) who represent the United States on the international circuit. Michael Matz has won many championships and grand prix events at home, and he first entered the European circuit in 1974.
In common with Canada and Australia, American riders have to contend with very much greater distances if they are to compete on the international circuit which tends to center on Europe. Canada's well-known Jim Elder still competes internationally from time to time and, of the newcomers, Mark Laskin seems set for success.

Australia
Long distances and quarantine laws hinder Australian showjumpers, but John Fahey nevertheless achieved

British Jumping Derbies and count-less grand prix competitions through the 1960s and 1970s – the Aachen Grand Prix in 1964 was not the least of his triumphs.

Italy
It was naturally in Italy that the full influence of Federico Caprilli's teachings and his advocacy of the forward seat in jumping were first felt. Certainly for the first twenty years of this century, Italian showjumpers were among the very best.
The two d'Inzeo brothers, Piero and the younger Raimondo, were the sons of Constante, a sergeant in the Italian Cavalry, who had been taught by the great master, Caprilli. Both brothers rose to fame in the 1950s with Piero, initially the more

came equal fourth in those Olympics. In 1973 he competed in many of the world class European shows and in 1974 went through to the final leg of the World Championship, in which the four competitors have to change horses. Simon became Olympic Champion in 1980 and is today one of the world's top half-dozen riders.
Lastly, the showjumping world is bound to hear more of France's top rider, Gilles Bertran de Balanda, and Switzerland's Thomas Fuchs.

Showjumpers on the international circuit are friends as well as rivals, shown here are:
England's David Broome (top left), Nelson Pessoa from Brazil (top right), Caroline Bradley
from Great Britain (center left), Hartwig Steenken from West Germany (bottom left) and
the United States' Michael Matz (bottom right).

272

Showjumping elicits a concentration and excitement that is almost as intense in the crowd as it is in the competitors.

Josef Neckermann

A dressage rider of world renown. The winner of several Olympic medals and holder of World and European Championships.

I have often been asked about the horses which have been dear to me in the last thirty years of active riding. They all had their strengths and weaknesses. What they had in common were their differences, their contrasting characters; they were of different blood and thus they varied in appearance and disposition. I should like to present four of them here with which I succeeded in winning medals in Olympic Games: There was Asbach, staid and reliable, who was disturbed by nothing, not even a heavy shower of rain which pelted down when we entered the dressage arena in Rome in 1960; not for so much as a fraction of a second did he lose his rhythm when, for example, he caught the fence with his left hindquarter in the piaffe.

On the other hand, Antoinette, a gray mare, was quite different: she was the prima donna who knew only too well how beautiful she was and – if treated inconsistently – would do what she liked with her rider. She proved her real caliber when, in spite of a raging thunderstorm and the threat of an earthquake, in Tokyo in 1964, she followed me obediently, let me guide her and, frightened as she was, completed the test without a fault, although she would have much preferred to bolt off blindly. The trust she placed in me, her rider, moved me deeply.

The gray Mariano, with whom I competed successfully in my third Olympic Games in Mexico in 1968, was the perfect gentleman – sensitive, clever and demanding. His dignity would not tolerate punishment. When I once lost my temper and gripped him tightly with the spurs, he bore me a grudge for the next two weeks. At the 1966 world championships in Berne Mariano, for example, he was incapable of producing a single change of leg in the warming up arena, but then in the Grand Prix and in the jump off he put on a brilliant performance and became the undisputed world champion.

My fourth Olympic horse was Venetia, obedient, well-behaved, actually with only average talent, but extremely hardworking. She made mistakes only because she wanted to do everything perfectly. In the 1972 Olympic Games she surpassed herself: she presented the world's competitors with a fantastic performance, which enlarged our collection of medals. During my whole riding life I have always tried to ride and train horses so that they master the difficult figures – but I have always allowed the horse to teach me, too. We trained and learnt from each other. I have endeavored to create and to find a symbiosis between horse and rider – two individuals of equal standing, united by sport. Only in this way can mutuality, trust in one another, complete harmony, the enjoyment of working together and thus – as the ultimate climax – outstanding performance and success come about.

Josef Neckermann

Dressage – Prec

ision and Grace

Dressage is, in simple terms, the comprehensive training of horse and rider in which natural balance and control of movement are the key factors. It is essentially a development of the classical horsemanship practised by European medieval knights and later by cavalry officers, and it is manifested at its highest level of proficiency in the haute école and airs above the ground executed by the Spanish Riding School of Vienna. The word dressage comes from *dresser* – the French meaning to train and the initial stages of dressage are indeed the training foundation of horse and rider.

In Britain, in past years dressage was traditionally regarded as "foreign" and "a fanatic prancing". The duke of Newcastle, in exile during the years of Cromwell's Commonwealth, taught riding in Paris and Brussels, where he became acquainted with the French supremacy in dressage. After the duke's return to England following the Restoration, he attempted to pass on to other riders what he regarded to be an indisputable skill. To dressage purists, Newcastle's instruction fell somewhat short of the accepted level of proficiency since he relied on the running rein (US: draw rein). This exerts a restriction upon the horse that is felt should not exist.

The duke's enthusiasm and belief in dressage, however, cannot be denied: "Some wag will ask, what is a horse good for that will do nothing but dance and play tricks? If these gentlemen will retrench everything that serves them either for curiosity or pleasure, and admit nothing but what is useful, they must make a hollow tree their house, and clothe themselves with fig leaves, feed upon acorns and drink nothing but water ... I presume those great wits *(the sneering gentlemen)* will give Kings, Princes, and Persons of Quality leave to love pleasure horses, as being an exercise that is very noble, and that makes them appear most graceful when they show themselves to their subjects, or at the head of an army to animate it." At the time, Britain's horsemen were gripped with an absolute passion for fox hunting and paid little heed either to Newcastle or to later teachers and trainers, with the result

Above: **Complete concentration is essential to ensure success in dressage. Pictured here is Olympic medallist Liselott Linsenhoff of Germany.**

that until the 1950s, dressage was little practised by British riders, particularly in competitive circles. Moreover, Britain's showjumpers were outshone for the first 20 years of this century by the Italians, taught according to Caprilli's principles, and then by the Swedes and Germans who both place a considerable emphasis upon the need for formal dressage training. Dressage training today is designed to develop – and in competitions to test – the horse's suppleness, steadiness, correctness in all the paces and maneuvers and its response to the aids. Changes of pace and direction, changes of hand, voltes (the describing of small circles of about 20 ft diameter) and changes of leg are included in a rigorous training that may take five years, or usually longer, to perfect. It is generally considered that a horse will compete at novice or preliminary stages for about a year, at Elementary for another year, Medium a third, and the Advanced movements for at least another two years. The FEI, which is responsible for the international rules of dressage, showjumping, eventing and combined driving, has defined the qualities required of the dressage horse: "Dressage is the harmonious development of the physique and ability of the horse. As a result it makes the horse calm, supple, confident, attentive and keen, thus achieving perfect understanding with the rider.

"These qualities are revealed by:
– Freedom and regularity of the paces.
– Harmony, lightness, and ease of the movements.
– Lightness of the forehand, and engagement of the hindquarters, origination in a lively impulsion.
– The acceptance of the bridle, with submissiveness throughout and without any tension or resistance.

"The horse thus gives the impression of doing of his own accord what is required of him. Confident and attentive he submits generously to the control of his rider, remaining absolutely straight in any movement on a straight line, and bending accordingly when moving on curved lines.

"His walk is regular free and unconstrained. His trot is free, supple, regular, sustained and active. His canter is united, light and

Below: **European cavalries have traditionally excelled at the exacting discipline of dressage.**

Above: **Obedience, intelligence and fluent movement are the prerequisites of the dressage horse. Competing here is Reiner Klimke of Germany.**

Above: **Josef Neckermann on
Duero demonstrates the close
rapport required between
horse and rider in dressage
competitions.**

cadenced. His quarters are never inactive or sluggish; they respond to the slightest indication of the rider, and thereby give life and spirit to all the rest of his body.

"By virtue of a lively impulsion and the suppleness of his joints, free from the paralysing effects of resistance, the horse obeys willingly and without hesitation, and responds to the various aids calmly and with precision.

"In all his work, even at the halt, the horse must be on the bit. A horse is 'on the bit' when the hocks are correctly placed, the neck is more or less raised, according to the stage of training and the extension or collection of the pace, and he accepts the bridle with a light and soft contact, and submissiveness throughout. The head should remain in a steady position, as a rule slightly in front of the vertical, with a supple poll as the highest point of the neck, and no resistance should be offered to the rider."

The secret of the top class dressage rider is to persuade the horse to perform in such a way that it looks quite natural and quite effortless. The well-collected horse is a delight to watch, even by the uninitiated. An excellent display of dressage can be compared with Olympic diving or gymnastics – performing the maneuvers at all takes some skill but to render a truly balletic, fluent display requires a complete and confident mastery of the discipline. The three best-known Grand Prix dressage movements are the piaffe; the pirouette, in which the horse pivots on its hindfeet as it circles; and the passage, in which the horse trots with a high, springy action, its feet momentarily suspended between each step. The haute école airs above the ground movements include the capriole, the ballotade, the croupade and the levade; the courbette in which the levade position is assumed prior to several leaps forward; the pesade, the preparation for the levade; and the passade in which the horse takes a minute turn with the hindquarters performing a smaller circle than the forequarters.

The world's top dressage riders include Christine Stückelberger, Britain's Jennie Loriston-Clarke, Germany's Schulter Baumer and the Russian's Elena Petouchkova and Ivan Kisimov.

Below: **To train a horse to top-class dressage standard can take many years and demands skill and patience.**

Above: **Regarded as one of the world's top dressage riders, Swiss Christine Stückelberger on Granat won the 1976 Olympic Games, the European Championship in 1977, and the World Championship in 1978.**

The criterion of dressage is harmony of movement. Gabriela Grillo riding Ultimo provides a fine example of a perfect team.

Above: **The Three-Day Event is a test of endurance and of skilled horsemanship, in which many riders have become household names. Among them are: Richard Meade (Olympic gold medallist), Sheila Wilcox (three-time winner at Badminton), Princess Anne (European Champion 1971), Captain Mark Phillips (Olympic Team gold medallist and three-time winner at Badminton), Lucinda Green (neé Prior-Palmer, European Champion and Badminton winner), Jane Holderness-Roddam (Olympic Team gold medallist and**

Speed and Endurance

Eventing has its origins in the training and exercises carried out by cavalry officers until the beginning of the twentieht century. The three-day event was known as *le Militaire* in France. The first Militaire took place in 1902 and just ten years later became part of the Olympic Games. Principal three-day events today include the Badmington Horse Trials held in spring each year, the Burghley Horse Trials held in the fall, the Pan-American Games and the US Horse Trials at Ledyard, and, in Australia, the Gawler Horse Trials. The highest acheivement for an event rider would, of course, be to take part in the Olympic Games where this great sport is featured. Eventing competitions today, or Horse Trials as they are sometimes called, may be held over one, two or three days. Some of the major three-day events in fact spread over to four or five days, but they are still referred to as three-day events. All eventing competitions comprise three main phases – dressage, show-jumping and cross-country jumping course. Competitors have to complete a long ride over roads and tracks intercepted by a steeplechase course – all of which must be ridden within a certain time limit. This is a great test of a rider's skill: he must know how fast to push his horse in order to complete just within that time limit. By finishing with only a few seconds in hand, he will have spared his horse as much as possible for the gruelling cross-country course ahead.

In a three-day event, the show-jumping is the final phase, and is designed less to judge the horses' jumping ability in the ring as to judge their overall fitness, stamina and precision after the all-out effort of the day before. In one-day and, sometimes, two-day events, on the other hand, the showjumping comes before the cross-country phase. In this instance, therefore, it becomes a test of the horse's ability to jump and spares those who fall by the wayside from attempting the altogether more solid and relentless fences of the cross-country course. Official events are divided into various categories, such as novice, junior, intermediate, open inter-mediate and advanced, according to the standard and official grading of horse and rider. Three-day events are subject to further and more

complicated categorization. In each category, there are strict specifi-cations governing, for example, the size of the fences in the cross-country and showjumping courses and the overall speed at which each section of the course must be ridden. The dressage test varies, too, according to the standard of the event; in a top-class event, it will last about 10 minutes, and there are further specifications as to the sort of tack and equipment that may or may not be used.

For more advanced events there are rigorous qualifying con-ditions for competitiors designed al-ways to ensure that no horse will be entered for an event really beyond his present capabilities.

twice winner at Badminton), Mary Gordon Watson (World Champion 1970), Bruce Davidson (World Champion 1974) and Tad Coffin (Olympic medallist).

Above: **The event horse must tackle formidable water jumps without hesitation. Most cross-country courses include a shallow river or lake.**

Spills are not infrequent in eventing, and it is often the water jumps that prove the most hazardous.

Lester Piggott

Great Britain's most successful jockey, having won every
major race in a career
spanning three decades.

The speed of the horse, whose natural
instinct is to flee, has, since time
immemorial, exerted a fascination on
man, and this found expression in
equestrian games and competitions
and especially in racing. But races
were not held for enjoyment alone.
They were a method of selecting the
fastest and toughest horses, which
were then used for breeding purposes,
so that their outstanding qualities
could be passed on.

This selection method has hardly
changed. The conditions of the racecourses around the world have
become a kind of scale for measuring
the performance of our Thoroughbreds. In our jet age, direct com-
parisons between horses from all the
continents have become a matter of
routine. Top racing horses are as
familiar with the atmosphere of the
airports as with the varying requirements of the race courses.

I am one of those people who have
made the world's most wonderful
unessential matter to their profession.

Admittedly, my family was long associated with the turf, both my father and my grandfather having been engaged in showjumping. Preparation for my profession began at the age of twelve. At sixteen I rode in Greece and from then on I made the rounds of the racecourses throughout the world.

My profession took me to all the great venues of international horse racing: to the flat, oval and pleasant-to-ride dirt tracks in the United States and the tricky race course at Longchamp in France; to the tracks in Japan with their crowds of spectators reminiscent of European football stadiums, as well as to Hongkong, Malaysia, Australia, India, Singapore, New Zealand, Jamaica, Puerto Rico, Venezuela, Argentina, Trinidad, to some African countries and, of course, to the great racecourses of Europe.

In the course of the years I rode horses which can be numbered among the really great ones in racing. Names like Nijinsky, Sir Ivory, an American-bred horse, are well known to fans of the turf. With them I won the Derby at Epsom and other famous races. Both were completely different horse personalities: Nijinsky moody and easily unnerved by any disturbance on the racecourse, Sir Ivory, on the other hand, placid and on the track full of irrepressible courage and will to win.

He achieved victories in Ireland, England, France and the United States, however unfavorable the going. Orsini earned my very special respect. He performed almost incredible achievements in series, running in races in quick succession, although the venues were a long way apart and he had to put up with arduous journeys by air or overland. My recollections of these three horses should also stand for all those I have ridden in races. They were all horse personalities, without whose individual qualities the fascinating atmosphere of the racecourse could never have arisen.

Lester Piggott

Racing – the

Sport of Kings

Horseracing is one of the most tense and exciting of all horse sports. It differs in a sense from showjumping, combined driving, eventing and dressage which could be described as international sports, in that it is really a huge and thriving industry. Betting, combined with the television coverage it has received since World War II, has exerted a significant effect on the racing business and value of race horses, which command enormous sums of money nowadays. For example, in 1979, a yearling was sold for US $

1.6 million to the Japanese, while three years before this, a colt had been sold for US $ 1.5 million. In such sales, much depends on the horse's breeding or pedigree, for colts and yearlings will not have proved themselves on the race track. Racing can be traced back to some 2500 years ago when the Mongols and the Chinese indulged in chariot racing. Horseback racing was included in the ancient Olympic Games held in Greece in about 550 BC. Horseracing today however, can be said to have descended directly from the sixteenth century

when it began in England partly as a response to or as a result of hunting. Those who rode to hounds wanted to test their horse's speed against one another and so indulged in various races. The development of selective breeding to produce good horses for the hunting field, particularly in the seventeenth and eighteenth centuries played a leading role in racing.

From these varied beginnings, several distinct categories of racing have developed: flat racing – by far the most popular and the most lucrative; hurdling – essentially racing on the flat, but over comparatively low obstacles; steeplechasing – racing over longer, more solid brush fences, epitomized by Aintree's Grand National; and trotting and harness racing. Trotting, is especially popular in the United States, France and Germany.

The British turf

As much as racing had been influenced by breeding and the search for fast and fearless horses for the hunting field, so this breeding eventually came to be dominated by the need for tireless race horses to meet the demand of the race track, to which the public

Above: **The tense moment before the start. Separated by only a matter of inches, the contestants wait in the starting boxes. The jockeys' faces are marked with concentration.**

flocked in their thousands. Neither breeding nor racing, however, came into its own until the development of the English Thoroughbred, now regarded as the world's supreme race horse.

The world's first known race track, the Smithfield, was established in London in 1174. Racing came to be known as "the sport of kings and the king of sports" with sound historical reason. Henry VIII imported horses for racing throughout his reign in the first half of the sixteenth century, and it was Charles II who revived and promoted a national interest in the sport. Racing was to some extent fostered as a social institution, being regarded as a lesser evil than conspiring against the king and rioting, both commonplace activities at the time. With Charles II's introduction of racing at Newmarket in the early 1660's, combined with his passion for the sport and the untiring search for better and better horses, the courses started by city corporations assumed a new vigor. Examples of such courses were to be found at Chester, Croydon and Salisbury. Charles II was himself an able horseman and frequently participated in races. Not only did he compete, he also made the rules (no others existed at the time).

Racing at Epsom was introduced in 1661. It was not until 1780, however, that the world's best known race, the Derby, was founded. Royal racing focused on Epsom and Newmarket through the reigns of James II and William III (who indulged in heavy betting). In the reign of Queen Anne, formal racing became established at York in 1709. The Queen awarded a Gold Cup for the winner of the four-mile heats. In 1711 the Queen, or her Master of the Horse, founded Ascot, and she offered the Queen's plate of 100 guineas the same year. The popularity of racing grew apace and with it betting flourished. Wagers were sometimes colossal and it was not uncommon for whole estates to be forfeited. Pepys declared: "Strange the folly of men to lay and lose so much money". Betting, it seemed, could get a grip on everybody for, at the other end of the scale, apprentices would wager their whole week's earnings on a horse. No rules

At the start of the race, horses and jockeys are huddled together. It will not be long before they begin to spread out.

These pages: **The horses need to clear the jumps by less than a hair's breadth as they race onwards. The higher a horse jumps, the more it will check its speed.**

existed about the running of a race and so all sorts of shady practices passed undetected. Feed and drinking water were doctored with poisonous plants before the race, or the horse given such drugs as were then available, including opium. All sorts of uncivilized maneuvers were seen on the track itself, such as one rider crossing right across the line of another.

In about 1750, however, the Jockey Club was set up primarily to arrange matches and to encourage prominent owners to meet, and to reform some of the more disreputable practices of the turf. The Jockey Club still controls the administration of flat racing in England today.

The second half of the eighteenth century saw the foundation of three classic races: Doncaster's St Leger in 1776, the Oaks at Epsom in 1779 and the Epsom Derby in 1780.

According to legend, the Earl of Derby and Sir Charles Bunbury tossed a coin to decide the name of the new race. Derby won the toss but Bunbury was to win the first race with Diomed – a stallion that was to achieve a lasting celebration in the history of American horse-racing.

The appeal of eighteenth-century racing in England was, if anything, eclipsed by that in the nineteenth. With the advent of the railway and better transport generally, races were better attended by a larger cross section of the public. With its increasing popularity, racing

Above: The racing silks, worn by the jockeys in owner's colors, enable spectators to identify their favorite at a distance.

The celebrated Grand National, held at Aintree near Liverpool, England, is as much a test of courage as speed. This daunting race with its huge fences yearly takes its toll of jockeys and horses.

Falls are frequent and sometimes fatal in this fast and dangerous sport. Most fences, however, are not solid and yield on impact.

became even more corrupt at all levels. Owners and trainers resorted to a variety of devious practises in order to win the "big" money. In 1830 the Derby alone was worth the then fabulous sum of £ 2,800. Despite the undercurrents, however, brilliant horses appeared with the Thoroughbred first becoming a recognized breed in 1793 and the word itself adopted from 1821. Thoroughbred breeding today is an international business, with a sire from one country frequently being put to a mare of another, while the progeny will race in a third country. The English Thoroughbred, there-fore, is to a great extent responsible for the international racing picture today.

The breed was exported to France from about 1830 – although racing had already become popular in the reign of Louis XIV (1643-1715) and during Napoleon's rule (1804-15).In the USA, racing was given a boost by the acquisition of the famous Diomed, who although considered past his peak, sired a number of excellent horses and founded the Lexington line.

Such was the pressure on English Thoroughbred breeders that some deterioration and reduction in the breed was noted in the earlier years of the twentieth century. After World War II, however, the industry received a new impetus with the advent of television which soon brought the sport into almost every home. The English betting shop became almost as popular as the pub – and on occasions such as the Grand National – established 100 years earlier in 1837 – even more so.

The United States

The North American Indians, with mounts stolen from the Spanish, soon discovered the thrills of racing against one another across the plains. The Spanish had already started to race in their native land, and it is likely that they took the sport with them to the American continent.

The settlers of the early seventeenth century made do with the very few horses that they could obtain either by infrequent import or by pur-chases from the southern American Indians. By the end of the century, however, racing was a popular sport. By the 1730's New York had at least three racecourses and it had earlier pioneered the town plates just a year after Charles II had done so at Newmarket.

Racing and match sprinting flourished through the nineteenth century with Kentucky taking over from Virginia and Maryland as the prime Thoroughbred breeding state. The Kentucky Derby was founded in 1875, the Jockey Club established in 1894 and American jockeys participated in British races from the 1890's.

The British soon discovered to their horror that the Americans were better jockeys, training methods were more advanced, and better facilities were available so that the horses were generally in superior condition. More attention was paid to shoeing and, on top of all this, the Americans were fervent

gamblers not – at the time – above doping their mounts to assure success. Doping became an offense only from 1904, but in any event the success of the Americans was mainly attributed to the fact that they rode with a completely different seat which made the horse's work much easier. The Americans won the Epsom Derby in 1901, 1902, 1903, 1905 and 1906, as well as scoring wins in innumerable other races on the British turf. The American riding seat, scornfully described as the "monkey up a stick", was largely responsible for the defeat of the English jockeys. The British still favored the hunting seat in which the rider sat

Key to some owner's colours

1	S.A. Aga Khan	
2	Schlenderhan	
3	Fernando de Alzaga Unzué	
4	Scuderia Castelverde	
5	H.M. Queen Elizabeth II	
6	Mr. John E. du Pont (Foxcatcher Farms)	
7	Mr. Alfred G. Vanderbilt	
8	Baron Guy de Rothschild	
9	Fährhof	
10	Mr. Michael Ford (Ford Stable)	
11	Mr. Bill Beasley	
12	The President of Ireland	
13	Mr. Charles E. Mather, II	
	(Avonwood Stable)	
14	Mr. Kazuo Fujii	
15	Mr. S. McGrath	
16	H.M. The Queen Mother	
17	Mr. Antony Imbesi	
18	Asta	
19	Mr. Harry F. Guggenheim	

42 Lord Donoughmore
43 Mr. C.T. Chenery
(Meadow Stable)
44 Baron Lunden
45 Mr. Mazaichi Nagata
46 Mme. R.B. Strassburger
47 Mrs. Richard D. du Pont
(Bohemia Stable)
48 Mr. Jack J. Dreyfus
(Hobeau Farm)
49 Mme. Cino del Duca
50 Bona
51 Major Dermot
McCalmont
52 Mr. T.L. Baillieu
53 M. Ernest Masurel
54 Sir Frank Packer and
Mr. L.K. Martin
55 Mr. Yuzaku Kato
56 Fohlenhof
57 Razza Dormello-Olgiata
58 Lord Derby
59 Mr. Rex C. Ellsworth
60 Mr. George Gardiner
61 M. Marcel Boussac
62 Mr. John Smallman
63 Mrs. Gerard Smith
64 Mrs. André Ozoux
65 Mr. and Mrs. H.F.
Oppenheimer
66 Ettore Tagliabue
67 Lady Sassoon
68 Comm. Guido
Ramazzotti
69 Mrs. Edith W. Bancroft
70 Waldfried
71 Colonel Jorge Castro
Madero
72 Mr. Frowde Seagram
73 Werne
74 M. Jacques du Roy de
Blicquy
75 M.M. Janssens
76 Mr. John McShain
77 Messrs. A.R. and
G.A. Ellis
78 Mr. Kokichi Hashimoto
79 W. Eichholz
80 Razza di Rozzano
81 Ebbesloh
82 Max Bell of Calgary
(Golden West Farm)
83 Mr. Yuji Kuribayashi
84 Atlas
85 Félix de Alzaga Unzué

(Cain Hoy Stable)
20 Mr. Brian H. Crowley
21 Lady Eva Rosebery
22 Mme. F. Beauduin
23 Mr. John M. Olin
24 Mr. P. Dolt
25 Gräfin Batthyany

26 M. Jean Couturié
27 Mrs. Ewart Johnston
28 Buschhof
29 Lord Leverhulme
30 M. Paul Duboscq
31 Messrs. P.G., A.J.
and K. Stiles

32 Sir John Astor
33 Charlottenhof
34 Comte de Rivaud
35 Anne, Duchess of
Westminster
36 Baron de Crawhez
37 Zoppenbroich

38 Baron Louis
de la Rochette
39 Mrs. D. Thompson
40 Mr. Robert J. Kleberg, jr.
(King Ranch)
41 Sir Humphrey de
Trafford

far back in the saddle, his legs almost straight and somewhat oustretches, holding the horse on a fairly long rein. By contrast, the Americans from the time of Tod Sloan who won 43 out of 78 races in Britain in 1898 – crouched forward on the neck of the horse, with very short stirrup leathers, a pronounced bend to the knee and very short reins. This crouch seat was much ridiculed when first seen in England – but in no time at all it became the seat of all racing jockeys.

Once the British jockeys started to compete against the Americans on their own terms, i.e. riding in a similar style, American successes became fewer and the "invaders" began to concentrate on their home tracks. The American anti-gambling laws of 1908, however, ensured that American owners and jockeys would still travel to English races. In 1913, Britain passed the Jersey act which meant in effect that many American horses could not be admitted to the General Stud Book – a severe blow to the American

racing fraternity. With the acquisition of Thoroughbreds from abroad, however, and more careful control in breeding, American racing flourished to become the thriving home industry it is today. American bred Thoroughbreds are exported all over the world and racing, under the auspices of the Jockey Club and the Thoroughbred Racing Association (founded 1942), has become one of the most popular sports in the United States. American racecourses are mostly dirt tracks of one mile or a mile and a furlong (one-eighth of a mile) length. Belmont and Aqueduct have turf courses within the dirt tracks and the Washington, among others, is a turf course. Belmont, 20 miles outside New York, is the home of the Belmont Stakes, the final leg of the American Triple Crown, and has seen some of America's supreme horses race to victory. Man O'War, one of the all time great race horses, won at Belmont in 1919 by six lengths, before running nine more as a two-year old and losing only once. He won all his 11 races as a three-year old. In

1973 Secretariat took the Triple Crown with a victory at Belmont of 31 lengths. Of the United States' many racecourses, Churchill Downs – home of the Kentucky Derby – Santa Anita, Aqueduct, Pimlico, Keeneland, Hialeah, Hollywood Park and Saratoga are just a handful of the most spectacular. Churchill Downs is a dirt track circuit, which opened in 1875, the inaugural year of the Kentucky Derby. For its major races, the course attracts over 100,000 spectators. In 1973 Secretariat set the Derby record at 1 minute 59 seconds over the course – a speed equivalent to nearly 38 mph (60 km), over a track recognized for its difficulty. Aqueduct was completely rebuilt in the 1950's at a cost of US $ 33 million. Opened in 1959, it is distinguished by being only 12 (20 km) miles outside Manhattan, by having its own subway station and by its capacity to take at least 80,000 at year-round events. Maryland's Pimlico track is in the heart of traditional racing country and is the home of the Preakness, the second lap of the Triple Crown.

The race gets its name from the horse called Preakness, winner of the inaugural race in 1870 – later to be shot by his subsequent owner, the Duke of Hamilton, in a burst of rage at the horse's consistently unlovable disposition. Pimlico has seen many a dramatic spurt of speed, but it is again Secretariat that is the most memorable. Towards the end of the 1873 Preakness, this awesome chestnut broke from the back of the field galloping up to win. Los Angeles has two famed racecourses in Santa Anita and Hollywood Park. These courses have the highest attendance and highest betting figures of anywhere in the States. Santa Anita, opened in 1934, pioneered the two features it is now difficult to imagine racing without: the photo finish and the magnetic control starting gate.

The United States is without doubt the foremost racing country in the world. Jockeys from Europe frequently visit the States in the international tradition established at the beginning of this century, in the same way that American jockeys continue to compete in Europe's prominent events.

Canadian Racing

Canadian racing started only at the beginning of the last century, the first recorded race being held in the 1820's in Montreal. Steeplechasing became popular by the middle of the century. Participants were initially reliant on American imported stock for their mounts, but breeding has finally come into its own in the last 50 years. Canada's harsh climate does not altogether encourage Thoroughbred breeding, but some successful horses have emerged nevertheless. Canada's chief course is the Woodbine, near Toronto, at which many prestigious races are held including the Canadian International Championship and the Queen's Plate Stakes, initiated by Queen Victoria.

European racing

England, Ireland and France are the three chief racing countries in Europe today. England, with its long history of horseracing, not only has Epsom, Newmarket, York, Ascot – the Crown racecourse – among its many established courses, but the renowned steeplechase courses of Cheltenham and Aintree. Cheltenham's Gold Cup was established in 1924. This prestigious trophy was won five years running by Golden Miller and by the immortal Arkle three years running.

The Grand National at Aintree Liverpool, is probably the most daunting steeplechase course anywhere – comprising as it does, 30 formidable obstacles, including the notorious Becher's Brook. It was so named by Captain Becher who, after total submersion in the brook, pronounced water without brandy to be even more unpleasant than he had feared! Run every March, almost without break since its inception in 1837, the Grand National attracts runners from all over the world with a colossal attendance and television audience. Only a handful of the starting field normally make it to the finishing line, and it was only in 1982 that a woman, Geraldine Rees, completed this formidable course for the first time. Royal Ascot is the highlight of the English social racing calendar, just as it has been since its foundation by Queen Anne in 1711, through the grandeur of the Victorian meetings and the elegance of the Edwardians.

Dress at Royal Ascot has always been almost as important as the races themselves. Rules are strict but they scarcely check the more exotic creations of the extrovert. Women were not allowed to wear trouser suits until 1970 and men still wear full morning dress.

Ireland has a tradition of horse racing older than any other country. Racing was known at the Curragh, one of the most famous racecourses in the world today, from the third century. Towards the end of the seventeenth century, it was reported that the turf was much superior to that of Newmarket's and the climate equable. By the 1850's, when racing was thoroughly subscribed and patronized by overseas owners and jockeys, the Curragh still held the four-mile races (6 km) that had formerly characterised English racing, but which had mainly been replaced by shorter sprints.

The Irish have a long tradition of producing magnificent horses. Irish hunters are considered by some to be second to none. The British

Household cavalry get their horses almost exclusively from Ireland and many of the world's most successful showjumpers come from the Emerald Isle. In the last 150 years, the Irish have also produced outstanding Thoroughbreds. The Curragh is now the home of the five Irish classic races, the Irish 2,000 Guineas Stakes, the Irish 1,000 Guineas Stakes, the Irish Derby, the Oaks and the St Leger, attended by owners and jockeys from all over the world. Phoenix Park – a particularly fast track outside Dublin – and Leopardstown – with year-round racing – are just

two of Ireland's many other racecourses.

In France, Napoleon set the seal on the development of racing with his imperial decree of 1805 that from 1807 races should be held, that prizes should be given and that the entire business should be under government control. Racing and breeding flourished and English Thoroughbreds were imported to improve stock. French steeplechasing is said to have been introduced from Leicestershire where Monsieur de Normandie regularly hunted. De Normandie was an influential horseman and a winner of an impromptu race at Chantilly before it became one of France's premier racecourses. Today French Thoroughbreds are of the highest quality, and they win cups and trophies at racecourses all over the world.

France's main racing events are

Above: Horseracing today is big business with thousands of spectators all anxious to secure a good position – and make their fortune by backing a winner.

Above: **Horseracing is one of the most popular of all spectator sports. Television has greatly increased its audience.**

Longchamp's Prix de l'Arc de Triomphe, Prix Vermeille and Grand Prix de Paris; Chantilly's Prix du Jockey Club, France's oldest race, founded in 1836, and the Prix de Diane; and Deauville's Prix Jacques le Marois and the Prix Morny. Longchamps and Chantilly are two of France's oldest and most prestigious courses, both near Paris, while the fashionable Deauville is on the north coast, south of Le Havre, and is the site of the premier French yearling sales.

Britain and France have largely dominated European racing and Thoroughbred breeding since the dawn of the sport in those countries. Attempts by German breeders to produce world class race horses have been severely hampered by the effects of two world wars, and it was clear in the 1970s that they were still not in the same league. Spain has never had a particularly strong tradition of racing, although racing was known in that country from the seventeenth century. It is Italy that provides the exception to British and French domination of the European scene. British and French races are the most demanding and consequently the most prestigious for the winner, but Italy has produced Thoroughbreds of great quality since the beginning of this century. One man, Federico Tesio, was responsible for this revolution in Italy's bloodstock. Tesio devoted nearly 50 years to the upgrading of Italian stock with imported stallions, and he also believed in the policy of sending his mares abroad to be covered. Tesio acknowledged the demands of the British and French tracks, sending his Thoroughbreds to compete in international races at Longchamps, Chantilly, Newmarket, Goodwood and Epsom.

Australia

Racing in Australia got off to a slow start, not least because there was a

Above: **Although most jockeys are men, women are now accepted in some countries.**

A day at the races in England still sees the rich and leisured classes in full force. The event often resembles a fashion show!

run nearly every day of the year. Prize money was high, the crowd enormous and betting colossal. Flemington, along with many other Australian tracks, is still very successful today – and 100 years ago was considered far superior to anything that Britain had to offer. By the end of the ninetweenth century, racing was tremendously popular all over the Australian continent, the horses were good, the stakes high, the betting avid and the standard world class. Steeplechasing had developed side by side with flat racing, with the Australian horses displaying a natural flair for jump-

ing, but it declined in popularity after the First World War, and flat racing became even more popular. Quarantine laws prevail against competition from North America and Europe, but Australia's parity with the international standard has meant that Australian jockeys compete – and win – in the northern hemisphere.

The racehorse
The multi-billion dollar industry of horseracing rests with the breeder, owner, trainer and jockey, all of whom dedicate themselves to the Thoroughbred.

dearth of suitable horses until the last century. With its colonial expansion all over the world, Britain introduced horseracing not only to Australia but all over the Far East – to Hong Kong, Peking, Shanghai, Singapore and Malaya, for example. British cavalry officers first raced in Australia in 1810 and just 10 years later the sport became established. Now it is immensely popular and among the most flourishing of all businesses. Australia's Ascot was established in 1840 and today is the home of such races as the Perth Cup, the Australian Derby and the WATC Derby. The same year saw the founding of Flemington, Australia's prime racecourse, followed by Rosehill in 1855, Caulfield with the world class Caulfield Cup in 1858, and Randwick with the Doncaster Handicap, Sydney Cup and AJC Derby in 1860.
Flemington, just outside Melbourne, lists among its many notable events the Melbourne Cup, the Victoria Derby, the Queen Elizabeth Stakes and the Queen's Plate, and the Australian Cup. The Melbourne Cup is the most popular race of all and the country practically comes to a standstill while it is underway. Flemington was conceived at the outset as a premier course with exceptional facilities. Twenty years after its foundation, it dominated the Australian racing scene with races

This page: **Between the thrills of the sporting event the motto is "See and be seen". The big races throughout the world are the meeting places of high society and constitute a** social event which is not to be missed. Only very few of those who go to the races have anything to do with horses in their daily lives.

Below: **A gleaming trophy symbolizes a victory that may well be worth a small fortune in prize money.**

What is looked for first in the race horse is a superb, if not ideal, conformation for without this balance and speed will be impaired. After conformation comes general appearance – alertness and a good eye being considered particularly important. Temperament perhaps comes last in the priorities. A buyer will often make his purchase at the yearling sales so he will not be able to assess performance on the track. He will therefore watch the horse carefully in all its gaits to see how it moves. Ease of action and a good

stride are the things he will be looking for. That temperament is less important in the race horse than in horses wanted for other disciplines is just as well: Thoroughbreds are often nervy and excitable and a minority can be downright vicious. It should, of course, be said that many have equable and lovable temperaments, too! The overriding factor of the race horse is of course performance – getting the horse to the start of the race and riding it to win is what racing is all about.

Breeding

In the early days of racing, owners bred and raced their own horses. Owner-breeders were still commonplace in the last century, but in the twentieth century breeding has become established on a sound commercial footing with the majority of owners buying their horses as yearlings and giving them

over to trainers who will prepare them for their racing career. Many trainers advise on the purchase of these yearlings, too. The most important sales include Keeneland's in Kentucky, Fasig Tipton's Saratoga Sales, Deauville's, Tattersalls' Houghton Sales and Goffs' Kill Sales in Ireland. A Thoroughbred becomes a yearling on its first January 1 or August 1 in Australia, so breeders are careful not to produce foals just before January 1 – or else that animal will shortly become a yearling while it may be only a month or two old. Clearly it is nowhere near ready for training and racing.

The days of the owner-breeder-rider such as Lord Derby are gone, and today an owner's prime requirement is wealth. The risks and hazards of horseracing are high: only a small number of yearlings eventually prove their value, and before they ever get to the track the trainer has to devote long and patient hours to them in a rigorous training schedule. Preparing a horse for the rigours and skills of racing, getting him to the peak of fitness is carried out either on special "gallops" near the training stables or in American racing in particular on the course itself. Training programs vary from country to country and from trainer to trainer, but they will depend on the type of race chosen for that particular horse.

The Jockey

The professional jockey has existed for about the past 150 years, and today trainers choose their jockeys either from those attached to the stables or from the list of those who operate on a freelance basis. Jockeys in Britain have traditionally been attached to one or possibly two stables, but the number of freelancers has been growing since Lester Piggott broke the accepted pattern many years ago. In America, however, jockeys are normally freelance, and they employ agents to secure them rides.

American jockeys in particular often work desperately hard (there are some 70,000 races a year) because the job is both extremely competitive and not always longlasting. For the European jockey, rigorous training starts in the spring when he may have to get his weight down by as much as 20 to 30 lbs if

These pages and overleaf: **The races held on the beach at Cuxhaven, northwest of Hamburg on the German coast, are no less exciting for spectator and competitor than conventional meetings on the turf.**

These pages and overleaf: **The winter races at St Moritz, Seefeld and Arosa give horseracing a romantic dimension. The unpredictabili-ty of the course is a keynote in these spectacular racing events.**

he has had an indulgent winter! Many jockeys stand at little over 5 feet and most are slightly built, but it is vital for them to be fit and lean for racing is an exhausting sport and a tired jockey is a positive hindrance to even the most energetic race horse. Those jockeys who work the year round have to watch their weight daily and must always be extremely fit.

A man's physical peak is considered to come about the age of 18, a woman's slightly later, but the records show that age is not always the determining factor in a jockey's success. American Frank Wootton made his debut at the age of 9, while many jockeys continue to race well into middle age. The winner of the 1982 Grand National – perhaps the most strenuous race of all – was aged 48! Clearly, experience is just as valuable. The outstanding jockey of the century was Canadian-born Johnny Longden who competed from 1927 to 1966. In that time Longden rode 6,026 winners, an all-time record until deposed by Willie Shoemaker. Britain's Gordon Richards was competing at about the same time (from 1920 – 1954) and his record of 4,870 winners was surpassed only by Longden. Not long short of Richards' record however, was the American Eddie Arcaro, whose 4,779 winners between 1932 and 1961 included five Kentucky Derbies and two Triple Crowns. Willie Shoemaker is today the most successful jockey of all time: by 1979 he had won US $ 75 million in nearly 8,000 races which included three Kentucky Derbies. Shoemaker stands at just 4'11" and weighs about 100 lbs. The lightest jockey of all time was Kitchener, the British jockey who competed in the mid-nineteenth century: in 1844 he won the Chester Cup weighing 49 lbs. Lester Piggott is without doubt Britain's outstanding jockey. Winner of the Epsom Derby eight times, Piggott was the British Champion in 1960 and then again, six times running, from 1964 to 1969. His many wins include the Prix de l'Arc de Triomphe three times, the Irish Derby four times and the German Derby three times. Although Piggott has competed less often in the last ten years, he is still much in demand as a champion jockey.

The American, Steve Cauthen emerged at the end of the 1970's as a new champion jockey, taking the American Triple Crown in 1978. His move to Europe in 1979 was marked by winning the 2,000 Guineas at Newmarket in England. The Queen's jockey, Willie Carson, has been British champion jockey three times from 1972, the first serious challenger to Lester Piggott. Carson is noted for his indomitable will and determination to win. In 1981 he suffered a fractured skull, but in May 1982, on the day that he got married, he came back to

compete in the Chester Oaks. Walter Swinburn, a former champion boxer, was Irish champion jockey in 1976 and 1977 despite hot competition from Tommy Carberry. Carberry set a record in 1975 by winning the Cheltenham Cup, the Grand National and the Irish Distiller's Grand National.

Swinburn became the youngest jockey in 1981, at 19, to win the Epsom Derby since Piggott's memorable 1954 win at the age of 18 on Never Say Die.

Australia's Roy Higgins has won the Victorian Jockeys' Championship no less than 11 times as well as practically all the prestigious Australian races, including the Melbourne Cup twice. Harry White, another outstanding Australian jockey, has won the Melbourne Cup four times and the Victorian Jockeys' Championship three times.

Racing is an international sport – and a world-wide business. The Epsom Derby, which has produced distinguished descendants all over the world – the Kentucky Derby, the Australian and Victoria Derbies, the Irish Derby (first known as the Irish O'Darby), the French Derby, the Derby Italiano and the German Derby – remains the world's premier race. The 1981 winner, the Irish-bred Shergar ridden by Ireland's Walter Swinburn, collected $ 270,000 for his owner. The 1982 winner, Golden Fleece collected $ 264,000, proof that racing is in a different financial league to other equestrian sports.

Skikjöring is for the really adventurous. Competitors have to be not only proficient skiers but also highly skilled in harness racing.

Stanley Dancer

A name synonymous with the sport he dominates. Winner of over 3,500 drives, including the sport's most prestigious races. As a trainer, four of his horses have won seven Horse of the Year titles, whose 1:56 4/5 minute mile on a half mile track at Saratoga Harness in 1969 still stands and is predicted to be a mark that will last for ever.

Harness racing, a sport in which horses compete on the trot or pace is a sport indigenous to the United States, as the Standardbred was developed as a breed and exported to other countries.

The origin of the modern trotter and pacer in the United States can be traced to the importation in 1788 of an English Thoroughbred named Messenger. Although Messenger was an important factor in the development of the American Thoroughbred, his enduring fame is as the founder of the American Standardbred race horse. Today, almost all American Standardbreds are descended from Messenger. When the gray stallion died in 1808 on Long Island, he was given a funeral with full military honors. There is a monument at Messenger's gravesite, the last line of which reads: "None but himself can be his parallel." Today Messenger is honored by the Messenger Stakes, a leg of the Triple Crown of pacing contested at Roosevelt Raceway on Long Island.

Although Messenger is the father of the American Standardbred, it should not be inferred that trotting and pacing was born with the influence of

Messenger. Trotters and pacers have actually been mentioned in literature and history for centuries. Xenophon (430-355 BC), in his *Art of Horsemanship* discussed the walk, trot, and gallop. It is believed that the pacing gait was unknown to the Greeks until some point after the time of Aristotle (384-322 BC), who wrote that if a horse moves the two legs on the same side at the same time (the pacing gait), he surely must fall down.

But if the Greeks did not yet know of pacers, other contemporary cultures most certainly did. The pacing gait was represented in Assyrian, Egyptian, and Phoenician art and on vases and coins. Mention is made of a Spanish breed of horses whose natural gait was the pace.

Horses are shown on the trotting and pacing gaits in the famous Elgin marbles, the marvelously preserved friezes from the Parthenon in Athens exhibited in the British Museum. Leonardo da Vinci sketched horses in trotting and pacing motion.

In England, the Norfolk breed of trotter and the Galloway pacers from Scotland, as well as the Hobies, also pacers, from Ireland, were famous as coach horses during the American Colonial period.

Just before the importation of Messenger, the New England colonies, particularly Rhode Island, developed an outstanding breed of pacers known as the Narragansett. It is accepted, almost beyond any doubt, that Paul Revere rode a Narragansett pacer on his memorable ride on the evening of April 18, 1775.

From a horse named Hambletonian, a highly inbred great-grandson of Messenger, descend almost all of today's trotters and pacers in the United States and Canada, as well as most of those in Australia and New Zealand. Hambletonian blood also plays an increasingly important role in the development of the European breed of trotters. It should be noted that over forty nations have trotting and pacing races. Today, Hambletonian is immortalized by the Hambletonian Stakes, the most prestigious of the trotting Triple Crown events. The Hambletonian is now raced each August at the Meadowlands Race Track in New Jersey, U.S.A.

Stanley Dancer

Trotting and Pacing the Modern Charioteers

The comparatively recent sports of harness racing and trotting and pacing races are closely related in origin. It is something of a phenomenon that these sports should have achieved such undeniable popularity, owing nothing as they do to the technology of the twentieth century and everything to a bygone age.

Trotting races, both ridden and harness, started to become popular in the United States and Europe from the beginning of the nineteenth century. With the invention of the light carriage, the sulky, harness racing quickly became increasingly popular – particularly in the United States where, by the 1850s, ridden trotting races were so far superseded by harness events that all trotting became generally known as harness racing. In Europe, saddle trotting remained popular through the nineteenth century and still does

today, notably in France, Belgium, Germany and also in Russia. Coaching and driving events, usually known as combined driving, also exhibit the unique high-stepping action of the trotter. Uniquely popular in England, coaching and driving events were known first in the eighteenth century. Their popularity increased with the invention of lighter carriages and with the ever more common sight of the mail coach teams. With the advent of the railways, mail coaches became obsolescent and coaching and driving events became, for a time, less popular. Since the Second World War, coaching and driving has enjoyed a tremendous revival with Prince Philip's declared enthusiasm. The British Driving Society was formed in 1957, and from 1964 it has held its own show in the grounds of Windsor. International competitions started in the early 1970s – and Britain has been represented by Prince Philip and by the doyen of driving, Cynthia Haydon, among a host of other distinguished contestants.

Of all the competitive driving events, however, it is American harness racing that has dominated both harness racing and trotting. The "Yankee" trotters, as they were known, were found to be the best for these types of events and this is largely because they contained a higher proportion of Thoroughbred blood. The Narragansett Pacer – now no longer in existence – and the Standardbred, both described in the introduction to this chapter proved to be the breeds that set American harness racing on its course. The term "Standardbred" did not appear until the early 1880s, but within 10 years the breed was an attractive alternative to the pacer – with its distinctive lateral gait in place of the normal diagonal gait – despite the fact that the pacer was faster.

Today the Standardbred is the star of American harness races. The Standardbred was introduced into France in the nineteenth century and also there became a dominant breed in trotting races.

In Europe, it is the French Trotter and the Russian Orlov Trotter that are used in trotting races, while the Hackney in England is the archetypal horse for coaching and driving.

Above: **A field of trotters' fans out for the homestretch and the drive to the finish line.**

Above: **Ever since there have been harness races, they have been exceptionally popular and a paradise for gamblers as well. Harnessed to the** **sulky, a light two-wheeled carriage, the horses develop top speeds of over 30 mph (50 km).**

Above: **A special atmosphere of excitement surrounds the staccato of the hoof beats and the field of horses and sulkies lying so close together. A clear view and fast reactions on the part of the drivers are important in determining the outcome.**

American harness racing

The lightweight sulky, invented in 1804, revolutionized American harness racing despite fervent protests by more traditionally minded enthusiasts. In the 1830s and '40s, Americans adopted their first sports heroes – the immortal trotter, Lady Suffolk, was the first to better the 2.30 minute for the standard mile distance. Lady Suffolk rode 50 races under the saddle and then was turned to harness in which she trotted 112 races with her trainer driver, Hiram Woodruff, of whom, it was said: "drove so beautifully as to abate the usual ridicule of the vehicle." (The sulky was yet to gain full acceptance.)

Harness racing in America steadily

champions seen in an even better light, when it is realized that in this pre-automobile era there were no horse vans; these great trotters were their own means of transportation from track to track. Driver, wagon, and equipment were all pulled to the next stop on the circuit by the very animal upon which all this effort was expended. Goldsmith Maid in particular gained a degree of notoriety for her exploits at various tracks separated by (at that time) great distances, often only two or three days after racing at her previous stop.

It was with the turn of the century, and the advent of the automobile, that harness racing was toppled from its perch atop the American sporting scene. The revolution

he ever competed, Dan Patch paced the mile in 1:55 1/4 minutes in 1905, an effort years ahead of its time. Still an extremely fast mile, Dan Patch's record was not broken until Billy Direct lowered it to 1:55 minutes in 1938. A true American hero, the bay stallion regularly drew huge crowds wherever he went, once time-trialing for over 50,000 spectators at the Minnesota State Fair. Dan Patch travelled from track to track in his own private railroad car and his name became familiar to everyone as the most common household items, including flour, baking soda, and children's sleds, bore his brand-name. At the end of his illustrious career, he went on to become a successful breeding stallion.

increased in popularity with meets held on an April through November basis. From the 1860s until the end of the century, the popularity of trotting was stimulated by a successive wave of champions, many of whom came to be household names. New favorites emerged as a parade of popular trotters followed Lady Suffolk as the equine ruler of their day – Dexter, Ethan Allen, Goldsmith Maid (winner of 350 races in her illustrious career), Flora Temple, and St Julian are just but a few of the famous names of the day.

The racing of the era can be viewed more romantically, and the

brought about by the "horseless carriage" changed not only the primary method of transportation for Americans, it changed an entire lifestyle as well. Less people owned horses and consequently harness and trotting races in particular declined.

Before harness racing fell from the public's grace it was to be blessed with one more shining star, an equine hero who was to achieve a level of fame that today's best known horses, Secretariat and Niatross, never came close to equalling. This was the American-bred Dan Patch.

The winner of every race in which

Above: **Only the toughest, the healthiest and those with nobility and courage can stand the test.**

347

Trotting at high speed is something that has to be learnt. The natural instinct to gallop has to be suppressed. A trotter that forgets this is disqualified.

These pages: **Seemingly weightless, unimpeded by the sulky and its driver, the competing horses appear as silhouettes in the evening twilight. In the U.S. and** **Canada there are many amateur drivers who, after acquiring the necessary competence, may race against professional drivers on the major tracks.**

During the period preceding harness racing's new rise to popularity as a nighttime, parimutuel (the American equivalent of the British Tote) sport, one other great hero demands a mention – Greyhound.

Racing for minute purses in the sport's darkest days during the Depression, the "Grey Ghost" etched his mane into the record books in over 40 places. Conqueror of every horse he ever raced against and winner of his Hambletonian race, Greyhound clocked the mile in 1:55 1/4 minutes in 1938. This stood as the fastest mile ever trotted for almost 31 years, until the great Nevele Pride outshone him in 1969. Even 44 years later, only five times has the mile been trotted faster than Greyhound's epic record! An exquisitely bred horse, Greyhound was gelded while a young colt and the sport never benefited from his presence in the stud.

The renaissance of trotting

After floundering for several decades as a minor sport, of interest only to country farmers perhaps, harness racing was revolutionized and rejuvenated by the foresight and courage of a Long Island attorney named George Morton Levy. Against the advice of just about everyone, Levy and a small group of investors began construction of a major-league harness track in Westbury, Long Island. Levy felt that the combination of nighttime racing, parimutuel wagering, and aggressive promotion could provide the ingredients for an American trotting renaissance. And so Roosevelt Raceway was founded on September 2, 1940.

After several years, the sport began to catch the fancy of New Yorkers and Roosevelt Raceway became a profitable investment. Other parimutuel tracks sprung up in the wake of Roosevelt's success and bigtime harness racing was reborn. Roosevelt's rapid ascent earned it the reputation of being the "World Capital of Harness Racing". Today it is home to the International Trot, as well as the Messenger Stakes, a leg of the pacing Triple Crown. Exactly 36 years after the birth of Roosevelt, a new giant opened its doors for harness racing for the first time. On September 2, 1976, over 43,000 people crammed into the

Meadowlands Racetrack in East Rutherford, New Jersey, to witness the opening of harness racing's new supertrack. It never will be known how many people actually attended that inaugural program because the track, filled to the limit, announced that no more fans could enter and closed the turnstiles, only to have a gate crashed through which at least several thousand more fans entered. Today, the Meadowlands regularly plays to crowds of twenty or thirty thousand which often bet upwards of three million dollars on a single card. What the track lacks in history or tradition it makes up for in money, as almost all the world's richest races are held at the supertrack. The $ 2,000,000 Woodrow Wilson Pace, and the $ 1,000,000 Hambletonian Trot highlight the Meadowland's staggering purse structure and has attracted North America's best horses and drivers. In addition to the three New York area tracks, harness riding also enjoys great popularity in Chicago (Sportsmans' and Maywood Parks), Toronto (Greenwood and Mohawk Raceway), Montreal (Blue Bonnets Raceway), Philadelphia (Liberty Bell Park, Brandywine Raceway), and Los Angeles (Hollywood Park and Los Alamitos Race Course).

The tremendous rewards generated by the parimutuel windows have fueled a booming market for Standardbred bloodstock too. Of 1981's six leading two-year-olds, four (Icarus Lobell, Merger, No Nukes, and Temujin) have been syndicated for upwards of $ 5,000,000. The two others (Ideal Society and McKinzie Almahurst) have been retained by their owners in the hope that successful three-year-old

campaigns will further increase their value.

The breed's leading stallion, Albatross, a former champion himself, now stands for a stud fee of $ 75,000 and his book is full and closed with over 100 mares. In 1981, sons and daughters of Albatross alone earned over $ 10,000,000 on North American race tracks. Yearlings and broodmares regularly sell for six-figure sums as owners compete to have the best quality horses for the big races.

The Triple Crowns

Just as is the case with its sister sport, Thoroughbred racing, harness racing has a Triple Crown series towards which all owners can aspire. The sulky sport has two Triple

Above: It requires exact timing and quick reflexes to maneuver the sulky out of the field of dashing horses into a strategic position to overtake.

Crowns, one for trotters and one for pacers.

The Triple Crown of trotting, inaugurated in 1955, has seen six great horses sweep the coveted series: the Hambletonian (Meadowlands Race track), the Yonkers Trot (Yonkers Raceway), and the Kentucky Futurity (Lexington Red Mile).

1955 Triple Crown champion Scott Frost accomplished his sweep at the expense of his ever-present rival, Galophone, who was second in the Hambletonian and the Yonkers. The winner of 56 of 71 lifetime starts (70 times one-two-three!) and $ 310,685, Scott Frost was voted in 1955 and 1956 Horse of the Year for trainer, driver Joe O'Brien.

It was to be eight years until Speedy Scot and trainer driver Ralph Baldwin repeated the hat trick in 1963. Speedy Scot was a lifetime winner of 44 of 57 starts, earning $ 650,909 and selection as 1963 Horse of the Year.

It was only the following year that Ayres turned the 1964 trick for trainer, driver John Simpson, Sr.. With 20 wins (27 times one-two-three) in 30 starts, Ayres banked $ 254,027 in his short career.

1968 winner Nevele Pride is arguably the greatest trotter since Greyhound. The winner of 57 of his 67 outings (64 times in the money) for $ 873,238, the Stanley Dancer trained and driven star is the only trotter to be voted Horse of the Year three times (1967, '68, '69). Still the fastest trotter in history with a 1:54 4/5 minutes clocking, his 1:56 4/5 minutes win over Saratoga Raceway's half-mile track is perhaps the world record furthest ahead of its time.

No trotter has won the Triple Crown since it was accomplished by Super Bowl, another Stanley Dancer charge, in 1972. The son of Star's Pride-Pillow Talk recorded his Kentucky Futurity victory despite receiving a flat tire *in each heat*, Super Bowl won 38 of 51 starts (48 times one-two-three) and earned $ 601,006 in a brilliant career.

The pacing Triple Crown was inaugurated in 1956. Consisting of the Cane Pace (Yonker Raceway, the only track to host both Triple Crowns), the Little Brown Jug (Delaware Iohio County Fair), and the Messenger Stakes (Roosevelt Raceway), it has also seen six

Above: **Whether in the glowing heat of a summer's day or the crisp cold of winter, whether by day or under floodlight, harness races are colorful and exciting events.**

Driving is a relatively new equestrian sport. The confident and perfect mastery of harnessing and driving can be learnt, but still remain an extremely difficult art.

champions in its history.

1959 champion Adios Butler was the first to turn the trick. Ironically, Adios Butler was voted Horse of the year in 1960-61, but not in his Triple Crown season, in which he only started nine times. The winner of 37 of his 50 lifetime outings (42 times in the money), Adios Butler banked $ 509,844 under the guidance of trainer Paige West and driver Clint Hodgins.

1965 was the year of Bret Hanover, who was almost unanimously considered the greatest pacer of the modern era until Niatross came along. Bret Hanover won 62 of his 68 starts (including a 35 race win

streak), and collected $ 922,616 in his career.

Like Lindy's Pride, 1966 champion Romeo Hanover (Dancer Hanover-Romola Hanover) raced under the shadow of a better-known contemporary. Though he lost only one start at three and compiled a lifetime record of 36 wins in 44 starts (42 times one-two-three), earned $ 658,505, Romeo was never selected as Horse of the Year. The world champion was trained by Jerry Silverman and driven by William Myer and George Sholty.

What 1968 champion Rum Customer (Poplar Byrd-Custom Maid) lacked in brilliance he made up for with consistency. The Billy Haughton trained and driven charge retired as the richest pacer of his time, banking $ 1,001,548 on a record of 52 wins in 141 outings.

In 1970, champion Most Happy Fella (Meadow Skipper – Laughing

Girl) accomplished his sweep at the expense of a crop that included Columbia George and Truluck. After winning the Cane in stakes-record time, trainer/driver Stanley Dancer publicly predicted the colt's Triple Crown sweep. Happy won 22 of his 40 starts (35 times in the money), and collected $ 419,033 in his short career.

The result of decades of breeding the best to the best came to fruition in 1977 when a broodmare named Niagra Dream gave birth to an Albatross colt later to be named Niatross. Niatross retired in 1980 amid universal acclaim as the greatest Standardbred of modern times and over $2,000,000 in purse winnings in just two seasons at the races.

As a two-year-old and 1979 Horse of the Year, Niatross won all 13 of his starts and hinted at his greatness by easily humbling otherwise top horses. As a three-year-old and 1980 Horse of the Year, Niatross visited the winner's circle following 24 of his 26 starts. Ironically, his only losses were in consecutive races. He paced the fastest mile ever raced (1:52 1/5 minutes) and stunned even his greatest fans by time-trialing in 1:49 1/5 minutes, the fastest mile ever paced. This bettered the previous record by just under three seconds.

American harness racing has so dominated the international picture, with the Standardbred achieving speeds comparable to the Thoroughbred on the race track, that it is really only France and Russia that can be said to compete on equal terms. France favors both ridden and harness trotting events, the most important being held at Vincennes – a course comparable with flat racing's Epsom – November through March. Although the French provide the Americans with serious com-petition in the World Champion-ships, it is the United States that consistently excel at a spectator sport that has outweighed even American football in its popularity.

Above: **Driving with several horses in harness requires the utmost understanding between the driver and his horses. Not only are they directed by the reins and the** **whip, but also by the driver's voice. Each horse knows its name; it reacts individually to rousing cries, reassuring encouragement or warning reproaches.**

The romantic atmosphere of the Wild West lives again when four-horse wagons thunder through the arena in the "Calgary Stampede" in Canada. This reckless style of driving often saved lives on journeys across Indian country. The mail coach (see following double-page illustration) is a reminder of past days.

Riding for Leisu

re and Pleasu

Thousands of people all over the world take part in the competitive equestrian sports – on a purely amateur basis. Many, many more, however, ride or hack just for the pleasure of riding a horse. For many people, watching professional show-jumping or racing is merely the next best thing to riding themselves, and they have no urge to achieve fame and success.

Riding purely for pleasure takes many forms from the simple hack to trail and long distance riding, western riding, rodeo participation, pony trekking, gymkhana events, sidesaddle riding. Vacation riding includes distance riding which may be trek and trail, the American cattle drive, in which you are really expected to pull your weight, covered wagon vacations following old western tradition, or Swiss, French or Irish horse drawn caravan holi-

days and pony trekking which is practiced in many parts of the world.

Leisure riding requires a sound, sturdy pony such as one of the mountain or moorland types or a reliable "hack". Hacks are generally thought of as being about 14.2 hands up to 16 hands, and their most desirable characteristic is an even, reliable temperament. Smaller mountain or moorland ponies, the Shetland in particular, make ideal mounts for small children.

The great popularity of riding among children, and especially girls, led to the founding of the Pony Club. The aim of the Club is to encourage horsemanship and appreciation of horses and ponies by organizing innumerable events. The word gymkhana derives from a Hindustani word related to games on horseback. Although they are indeed games, gymkhana events demand precision and speed in the young rider.

Gymkhana events include such games as musical chairs and apple bobbing and all sorts of team races and relay events. The bending race, which involves competitors weaving in and out of a line of poles is a perennial favourite. Among the funniest to watch is the team sack race in which the first competitor has to ride to a given point, dismount, climb the sack and then, leading his pony, jump and hobble back to the starting line. The second contestant of the team grabs the sack, gallops to the same point, dismounts, gets into the sack and then has to jump or hop home as quickly as he can, giving the sack to the third and finally the fourth members of the team before the game is won.

The United States have numerous different distance rides, the best known being the Trevis Cup named after the president of Wells Fargo, Lloyd Trevis. The Cup goes to the first rider to complete the 100-mile (160 km) trail – about a 24-hour ride. These long-distance rides are very strenuous and the rider has to spend long hours in the saddle riding over what may be extremely rough country. Great fitness and stamina are needed in both riders and horses. The best events are well organized, with vets, farriers and doctors manning the course.

Below: **With the growing demand for leisure time activities, riding has increased in popularity. It is a pastime appreciated by all ages.**

»And as I was riding along, my heart resounded in the lawn-dampened steps, resounded in the snorting and champing on the bit by my gray, and a blissful happiness lit up my heart and I knew: If I now dropped out of the world, I would fall into heaven!«

Baron von Münchhausen

These pages: **A young rider proudly presents his pony on his Sunday ride out. It does not have to be a Thoroughbred horse to provide the greatest happiness on earth.**

Pony trekking can be tiring but in no way does it compare with the gruelling competitive long distance ride. Although many adults enjoy these gentle riding treks, it is perhaps a pastime aimed mainly at children. The distances are much shorter with frequent rest stops. Distance or endurance riding probably originates with the cowboys of the Old West who had to travel with their herds of cattle over the huge, uncharted tracts of land of the United States. American cowhands today display their time-honored skills to the delight of audiences all over the States at rodeo and horse shows.

The first rodeo is thought to have been held in 1866 in Arizona, culminating 40 years later in the varied and colorful events of the American Wild West Show. Australia, too, organizes rodeo events for its 13,000 membership of the Australian Rough Riders Association.

The five principal rodeo events are calf roping, bull dogging or steer wrestling, broncobusting, bull riding and saddle bronco riding. All require a good measure of courage and dexterity. The intention in calf roping is to chase the calf and lasso it. Cowhands' horses are as skilled as their riders in this event, and the good pony will slither to a stop as soon as the calf is lassoed, pulling backwards so that the rope stays taut. As he does so, the rider dismounts and ties three of the calf's legs together to prevent its escape.

Bull dogging, or steer wrestling as it is sometimes known, is no doubt much more fun for the spectator then the competitors! The cowhand gallops into the ring towards the bull provided for the event. As he reaches it, he throws himself from the saddle and, grabbing the bull by the horns, attempts to wrestle it to the ground. Bull riding is no less hazardous; riders have to maintain their seat on the twisting animal for a minimum of eight seconds, and should they fall they have to escape the vicious horns.

Saddle bronco riding requires a determined rider who can hold his seat for ten seconds – contestants welcome the tougher pony because judges mark according to the performances of both horse and rider. In fact, riders wear spiked spurs to

incite further extremes of performance from the animal. Broncobusting is the classic rodeo spectacle, in which the contestant exerts the skill of years in his attempt to stay more or less seated, bareback, on the viciously bucking horse. All the contestant has for a hold is a strap in place of the saddle and the pony's mane. Eight seconds is the minimum requirement – but many fall short of this by seven seconds!

The professional riders of the rodeo ride western-style in the same way as the cowboys of the Old West. The style differs from the European style of riding in technique, but also in tack and clothing. It is closely related to distance riding today in North America and Australia and this is because it is a style that evolved in response to the long hours that had to be spent in the saddle. American horse shows include a western riding category in which there are sections for stock horse, dressage, trail horse, pleasure horse, parade class and cattle-working.

The western saddle has a deeper seat than the European saddle. In addition, it has a raised horn for securing the rope or lariat and a long leather flap to keep the rider's leg from continually rubbing the horse's sides. The stirrups are often made of wood or leather instead of metal so that they are not subject to extremes of heat or cold and they are sufficiently wide to accommodate the boot up to the instep. The saddle and stirrups are designed so that the cowboy has the firmest possible seat, leaving his arms and hands free for roping and lassoing. Western riding demands much of the horse; he must be well-trained, quick, responsive and intelligent. The well-trained western-style horse will anticipate and respond to the slightest movement of the rein. The rider holds the single reins high on a curb or bitless bridle, and as he moves his hands to the right, for example, the left rein just grazes the left side of the horse's neck – a sufficient aid for the western-trained horse to spin to the right.

Showmanship provides many children with their first sight of the horse – in the circus, at which riders of acrobatic ability can be seen performing spectacular feats of riding on superbly trained horses in an

These pages: **The horse can offer an unbeatable interest and sense of companionship.**

These pages and overleaf: **Trail riding is particularly popular in the United States, Canada and Australia where one can ride for days in a wild, free environment.**

atmosphere of glamor and excitement.

The circus, from its beginnings in the early eighteenth century in England and Vienna, was dominated by all manner of horse acts until the beginning of the twentieth century when the horse population was in general decline. Horse acts are still popular, however, at circuses all over the world. One of the earliest horse acts in the circus required the rider to leap off his galloping steed, explode through a suspended paper hoop and land on the horse's back as it galloped beneath the hoop. Hoops blazing with paraffin fires were soon introduced in place of the paper hoops to satisfy an audience keen to see more and more daring acts. From about the 1850s, American riders were jumping from the back of a galloping horse over a huge outstretched flag, held by four men at a height of about four feet above the ground, to land on the back of the horse. The flag could be up to 20 square feet.

Acrobatic horseriders soon discovered that audiences waited with bated breath for the possibility of a fall and before long the entertainers had perfected somersaults from the position of standing on the back of a galloping horse. This act was pioneered by the American Levi J. North, and it was another American, Robert Stickney, who perfected the double somersault on horseback. After that, leaping on and off and maintaining a balance with one foot on a galloping horse seemed child's play, and failed to capture the audience in the same way!

Circus horses have to be outstandingly calm and reliable, as well as intelligent so that they can respond quickly in the ring, whilst not being upset by the lights and the excited crowds. Horses have to be trained to respond to the rider's commands in the ring, and to perform alone with only the most discreet commands from the ringmaster. Dancing to music with pirouettes and other movements not unlike those of the haute école discipline have always been successful acts in the circus.

Classical horsemanship has played its part in the circus ring, with riders executing the levade, the capriole, the ballotade and other "airs above

the ground", all of which have originated in the Spanish Riding School fo Vienna. In addition to this, however, they also train their horses to perform other movements that come outside the "natural movements of the airs above ground".

It is a canter through the hills however, that still remains for many the ultimate in riding. The gentle enjoyment of the countryside and the matchless relationship developed with the horse beats all manner of entertainment or competition.

Index

A

Achetta ponies, 94
Akhal Teké, 213
American Quarter Horse, 150
American Welsh Pony, 176
American Wild West Show, 371
Andalusian, 83, 88, 168, 195, 203, 236, 244
Andean, 79
Anglo-Arab, 178, 184
Anglo-Norman, 184
Anne, Princess, 286
Appaloosa, 178, 184, 203, 204, 206
Arab horses, 71, 83, 108, 109, 116, 141, 168, 178, 187, 195, 207, 210–12, 170–1
Arcaro, Eddie, 335
Ardennes or Ardennais, 170, 184, 187
Assateague Pony, 82, 203, 204
Australian breeds, 213
Australian Brumbies, 73, 93, 94, 213
Australian horseracing, 323, 328
Australian Pony, 210
Australian Rough Riders Association, 371
Australian show-jumping, 271
Australian Stock Horse, 213
Austrian breeds, 194–5
Avelignese, 195

B

Bactrian, 70, 220
Badminton Horse Trials, 287
Balanda, Gilles Bertran de, 271
Baldwin, Ralph, 354
Barb, 83, 195, 171
Bavarian Warmblood, 192, 194
Belgian breeds, 184, 187
Belgian Heavy Draft, 184
Belmont Stakes, 320
Berber, 83
Boldt, Harry, 280
Bosnian Mountain Pony, 204
Bradley, Caroline, 269, 272
Breeding, breeds, 166–217
color and confor-mation, 170
racehorse, 171, 330
terms, 171
in the wild, 92–3, 108–11, 118, 122
Breton, 179, 184
Brinkmann, Hans-Heinrich, 259
British breeds, 176, 184
British horseracing, 298–9, 305, 312
British showjumping, 269
Broome, David, 164–5, 259, 269, 272
Brown, Buddy, 271
Brumbies, 73, 93, 94, 213
Budyonny, 213
Bullfighting, 220, 225, 236–7
Burghley Horse Trials, 287
Burma or Shan Pony, 230
Buzhaski, 220–4
Byerley Turk, 176

C

Calabrese, 195
"Calgary Stampede", 360
Camargue Pony, 73, 93, 102–3, 106, 116–17, 170, 205
Canadian International Championship, 321

Canadian racing, 321
Canadian show-jumping, 257, 271
Caprilli, Federico, 244, 256, 271, 281
Carberry, Tommy, 335
Carson, Willie, 335
Catlin, George, 136
Cauthen, Steve, 335
Cavalry horses, 70–1, 134–47, 152–3
Celtic ponies, 94, 103, 106
Chantilly, 321, 323
Chapot, Frank and Mary, 271
Cheltenham Gold Cup, 321
Chincoteague, 82, 203
Chupandos, 221, 224
Churchill Downs, 320
Circus horse acts, 375, 379
Cleveland Bay, 176, 194
Clydesdale, 168, 176, 179
Coaching and driving events, 344
Coffin, Ted, 287
Comanche Indians, 135, 136
Condylarthra, 62, 63
Connemara, 73, 109, 176
Coppe, Edward Drinker, 62
Cortes, Hernando, 83, 135
Costeno, 205
Cowboys, 150, 154, 214–15
Criollo, 178, 213, 230
Cross-country jumping, 287
Croy, Duke of, 94
Curragh, 321
Cuxhaven races, 331

D

Dales ponies, 73, 103, 176
Dancer, Stanley, 340–1, 354, 358
Danish breeds, 192
Danish Sports Horse, 192
Darley Arabian, 176
Dartmoor ponies, 73, 98, 99, 176, 205
Davidson, Bruce. 287
Derby, Epsom, 299, 305, 312, 313, 335
Devereux, Milton, 230
Distance riding, 366, 371
Domestic horse, 68, 70–1, 134
Dortmund horse show, 260–1
Draft horses, 70, 147–8, 150, 154, 170,-184, 192, 213
Dressage, 225, 244, 245, 278–85, 287
Dulmen, 93–4, 95, 96–7, 192
Dutch breeds, 187, 192
Dutch Thoroughbred, 187
Dutch Warmblood, 187, 192

E

East Friesian, 192, 194
Eastern European breeds, 210, 213
Edgar, Elizabeth, 269
Edgar, Ted, 269
Einsiedler, 194
Elder, Jim, 271
English Hackney, 178
English Thoroughbred, 176, 178, 203, 212, 299, 312, 340
Eohippus, 62, 63, 64, 65
Epsom, 299, 305, 321
Equus, 65, 68
Equus caballus, 68, 82
European Thorough-bred, 168
Eventing, 225, 286–93
Exmoor ponies, 73, 94, 98, 99, 176, 205

F

Fahey, John, 271
Falabella, 184
Falz-Fein, Frederic von, 73, 78
FEI, 257, 281
Fell ponies, 73, 103, 176
Fjord Pony, 86–7, 106, 168, 170, 192, 205
Flat racing, 296
Flemington, 328
Fletcher, Graham, 269
Forest horse, 68
Foxhunting, 238–41
Frederiksborg, 168, 192
Freiburger, 179, 194
French horseracing, 321
French Saddle Horse, 184
French Thoroughbred, 321
French Trotter, 184, 344
Frieseland (Friesian), 187
Fuchs, Thomas, 271
Furioso, 213

G

Galiceno, 203
Galloway Pacer, 341
Garrano Pony, 83, 203
Gawler Horse Trials, 287
Gelderland, 187
German breeds, 192–4
Germany, Jean, 269
Gidran, 213
Godolphin Arabian, 176
Gotland Pony, 83, 204
Grand National, Aintree, 298, 308, 312, 321, 335
Green, Lucinda, 286
Grillo, Gabriela, 284
Groningen, 187
Guerinière, François de la, 244
Gymkhana events, 366

H

Hackney, 176, 344
Hacks, 171, 176, 366
Haflinger, 93, 187, 190, 192–202, 204
Hambletonian Stakes, 341, 354
Hanoverian, 179, 192–3
Harness racing, 225, 298, 340, 344–59
Haughton, Billy, 358
Haydon, Cynthia, 344
Higgins, Roy, 335
Highland Pony, 73, 99, 108, 176
Hispano (Spanish Anglo-Arab), 203
Hodgins, Clint, 358
Holderness-Roddam, Jane, 286
Hollywood Park, 321
Holstein, 192, 193, 194
Horseracing, 171, 225, 296–339
Hungarian Breeds, 213, 216–17
Hunsterland ponies, 89–91
Hunting, 148, 220, 225, 238–41
Hurdling, 298
Huzula horses, 94
Hyracotherium, 62, 64

I

Icelandic ponies, 73–7, 83, 106, 192, 204
International Horse Show, Olympia, 256
D'Inzeo, Piero, 271
D'Inzeo, Raimondo, 254, 271
Irish horseracing, 321
Italian breeds, 195
Italian Heavy Draft, 195
Italian horseracing, 323
Italian showjumping, 271
Italian Thoroughbred, 323

J

Jenkins, Rodney, 271
Jockey Club, English, 305
Jockey Club, US, 313, 320
Jockeys, 330, 335
Jutland, 192

K

Kentucky Derby, 313, 320, 335
Kentucky Futurity, 354
Kisimov, Ivan, 283
Klimke, Reiner, 281
Knabstrup, 178, 192
Konik mares, 68, 94, 168, 210
Koof, Norbert, 269
Kusner, Kathy, 271
Kustanair, 178

L

Laskin, Mark, 271
Latvian, 213
Leopardstown, 321
Levy, George Morton, 353
Ligges, Fritz, 253
Linsenhoff, Liselott, 280
Lippizzaner, 168, 178, 194–5, 242–3
Lithuanian Heavy Draft Horse, 213
Longchamp, 323
Longden, Johnny, 335
Loriston-Clarke, Jennie, 283

M

Macken, Eddie, 264, 269
McNaught, Lesley, 269
McVean, Jeff, 271
Malapolski, 210, 213
March, Othniel Charles, 62
Matz, Michael, 271, 272
Meade, Richard, 286
Meadowlands Race-track, 341, 353, 354
Melbourne Cup, 328
Merychippus, 62, 64
Mesohippus, 62, 64
Messenger Stakes, 340, 353, 354
Military horses, 70–1, 134–47, 152–3
Missouri Fox Trotting Horse, 179, 203
Mongolian Wild Horse, 68, 82, 168, 220
Morgan, 178, 203, 210
Mould, Marion, 269
Murakoser draft horse, 213
Murghese, 195
Mustangs, 73, 78–9, 82–3, 88, 93, 94, 109, 136, 154–5, 205, 214–15
Myer, William, 358

N

Narragansett Pacer, 210, 341, 344
Nations Cups, 257
New Forest Pony, 98–9, 103, 109, 176, 204
Newmarket, 299, 321
Norfolk Trotter, 341
Noriker, 83, 178, 194
North American breeds, 203, 210
Noth American Indians, 83, 88, 135–6, 154–5, 312

O

Oaks, Epsom, 305
O'Brien, Joe, 354
Oldenburg, 187, 192, 193–4
Olympic Games, 135, 220, 253, 257, 287, 298
Orlov Trotter, 213, 344
Owen, Sir Richard, 62

P

Pacing, 340–1
Palomino, 179, 203, 205, 210
Percheron, 148, 168, 184
Peruvian horses, 79, 83
Pessoa, Nelson, 271, 272
Petouchkova, Elena, 283
Phoenix Park, 321
Phillips, Captain Mark, 286
Pigott, Lester, 294–5, 330, 335
Pineia, 204
Pinto, 179, 203
Plains Indians, 135
Plateau horse, 68
Plessippus, 65
Pliohippus, 65
Podhajsky, Alois, 244, 245
Points of the horse, 172–3
Polish breeds, 210, 213
Polo, 220, 225, 228, 229–31
Pony Club, 366
Pony of the Americas, 203, 204
Pony trekking, 366, 371
Preakness race, 320–1
President's Cup, 257
Przewalski's horse, 65, 68, 69, 71, 73, 78–9, 168
Pyrah, Malcolm, 269

Q

Quarter Horse, 203, 210
Queen's Plate Stakes, 321

R

Racehorse, 328, 330
Racing silks (colours), 305, 314–15
Rees, Geraldine, 321
Revere, Paul, 341
Rhineland, 192
Richards, Gordon, 335
Ricketts, Derek, 269
Robeson, Peter, 269, 271
Rodeos, 214, 225, 366, 371, 375
Roosevelt Raceway, 340, 353, 354
Royal Ascot, 299, 321
Royal Dublin Horse Show, 252
Russian Heavy Draft Horse, 213
Russian Trotter, 213

S

Sable Island pony, 203
Saddlebred, 203, 210
St Leger, Doncaster, 305
Salerno riding horse, 195
Santa Anita racecourse, 321
Saratoga Harness/Raceway, 340, 354
Schleswig Heavy Draft, 170, 192
Schockemöhle, Alwin, 30–3, 252, 259, 268, 269
Schockemöhle, Paul, 262, 268
Shagya Arab, 213
Shapiro, Neal, 271
Shetland Pony, 73, 98, 106, 168, 176, 203, 204, 366
Shire horses, 148, 170, 176
Shoemaker, Willie, 335
Sholty, George, 358
Showjumping, 225, 250–71, 287
Silverman, Jerry, 358
Simon, Hugo, 252, 271
Simpson, John, Sr, 354
Skelton, Nick, 269
Skikjöring, 335, 338
Smith, Harvey, 269
Smith, Melanie, 271
Smith, Robert, 269
Smith, Stephen, 269

Smythe, Pat, 269
Solosky farmhorse, 210
Sorraia pony, 203
Soviet breeds, 213
Soviet Heavy Draft, 213
Spanish breeds, 195, 203
Spanish Riding School of Vienna, 194, 236, 242–5, 256, 280
Standardbred, 203, 340, 344, 354, 358
Steenken, Hartwig, 269, 272
Steeplechasing, 321
Steinkraus, Bill, 269
Steppe horse, 68
Stückelberger, Christine, 283
Suffolk Punch, 176
Swedish Halfbred, 213
Swinburn, Walter, 335
Swiss Anglo-Norman, 194
Swiss breeds, 194
Swiss Halfbred, 194

T

Tarpan, 68, 70, 79, 82–3, 168, 210
Tennessee Walking Horse, 203, 210
Tersk, 213
Tesio, Federico, 323
Thiedemann, Fritz, 268
Thoroughbred, 171, 176
Thoroughbred Racing Association, 320
Three-day Event see Eventing
Trail riding, 366, 378, 380–1
Trakehner, 168, 175–6, 192–3
Trench, Charles Chevenix, 230
Trevis Cup, 366
Trotting and pacing, 208, 340–59
Tundra horse, 68, 106
Turkoman light horse, 220

U

Ukrainian, 213
US harness racing, 344, 347, 354
US horseracing, 312–13, 320
US Horse Trials, Ledyard, 287
US National Horse Show, 252–3
US showjumpers, 269, 271

W

Waler, 141, 213
Watson, Mary Gordon, 287
Weier, Major Paul, 253
Welsh Cob, 103, 106, 204
Welsh Mountain, 73, 99, 106, 176
Welsh Pony, 106, 176, 205
West, Paige, 358
West German show-jumping, 268–9
White, Harry, 335
Whittaker, John, 269
Wielkopolski, 210, 213
Wilcox, Sheila, 286
Wiley, Hugh, 271
Wiltfang, Gert, 252, 268
Winkler, Hans Günter, 248–9, 268, 269
Woodruff, Hiram, 347
Wootton, Frank, 335
Württemberger, 179, 192, 194

Y

Yakut horse, 68
"Yankee" trotters, 344
Yonkers Trot, 354
York racecourse, 299, 321

Afterword

Kurt Blüchel

Born in 1934, he has worked for many years as a publisher in the area of natural science. In addition to a series of remarkable non-fiction books, he has also published numerous illustrated volumes, including "The German Forest", "The Magic of Minerals", "The Healing Powers of Nature", "Germany, a Miracle of Nature" and "The Decline of Animals". At the end of 1980 he brought out the large illustrated volume titled "Wilderness Expeditions" by Heinz Sielmann.

I wanted to introduce the reader to the great, wide world of horses, to its beauties, its day-to-day routine and its unusual, its sublime and modest aspects. I wanted to show the horse as a part of creation which is worth preserving, with our help and vigilance; also to attract the attention of some authorities and owners of land and forests who lack understanding of the problem. For we have made such endless use of the horse – and continue to do so – both materially and mentally. As an English saying puts it: The earth would be nothing without man, but man would be nothing without the horse.

Much of what here for reasons of space could not be described by the author is to be found in the pictures. There, too, many readers will look in vain for their own particular concept of the horse. But to make up for this many photographs show new aspects, new attractions, new perspectives, especially where – as in the first part of this book – horses represent certain moods and feelings.

These and the other pictures are the most important part of this book. They show "a world of horses" in a very special way. And precisely that is the function of modern photography: to capture the fleeting moment, the irretrievable atmosphere, to show the essence and delight of life, with regard to both man and animals. For this reason, the technical means of expression are so important, in order to bring what we see closer, to emphasise it and to attract our attention to it. And behind the lenses and shutters are the people who are personally involved in making the illustrations. It is they, the photographers, to whom we all owe a debt of gratitude for this book. The best in the profession from all five continents placed over 48,000 photographs at our disposal, leaving us the agony of choice.

I should like to make special mention of three of the most outstanding horse photographers, on behalf of all who cooperated on this unusual volume.

First, there is the married couple Lída and Tomáš Mičel from a little village in the Tyrol. I have never before seen pictures which brought to life the essence of the horse in such perfectly beautiful and exciting scenes. What the two photographers have recorded with their motorised Canon cameras especially in Andalusia, on the Marbach stud farm and at the La Tour du Vallat biological staion – in the midst of the Camargue marshes in the south of France – can be admired in the first part of the book.

Thomas Zimmermann from Cologne, whose Leica turns equestrian sports into an aesthetic feast for the eyes, was also responsible for a considerable number of pictures in this book. More than 70 photographs are the result of his fascinating photo-art, for example the double-page illustrations on pages 274/275 (Fritz Ligges on Genius), 306/307 (steeplechase), 326/327 (top hat parade at Ascot) and 332/333 (galloping on the dunes).

I owe a very personal debt of gratitude to my daughter Cornelia, who as a passionate horsewoman managed to catch my publisher's eye for the wonderful world of horses. She represents all those millions of horse-lovers throughout the world who are normally ignored in books and pictures. Her Trakehner mare Sabischa is a horse like innumerable others, without any sporting ambitions, without acrobatic skills.

It is a horse that is never in the limelight of public attention, that does not jump over 6-foot high walls or a twelve-foot wide water jump, that does not go in for dressage and does not break any speed records on the race course. It carries its proud owner out into the country almost every day and provides her with happiness and relaxation in abundance.

List of Photographers

1: L. Miček; 2/3: L. Miček; 4/5: L. Miček; 6/7: T. Miček; 8/9: L. Miček; 10/11: L. Miček; 12/13: L. Miček; 14/15: T. Miček; 16/17: L. Miček; 18/19: L. Miček; 20/21: L. Miček; 22/23: T. Miček; 24/25: Image Bank/Sund; 26/27: Image Bank/Lomeo; 28/29: G. + J. – Fotoservice/Mangold; 30 o.: Peyer; 30/31: Cramm; 32 l.: Peyer; 32/33: Ernst; 34/35: Weiland; 36/37: Dossenbach/Minolta Team; 38 l.: T. Miček; 38/39: T. Miček; 40/41: Weiland; 41: Reinhard; 42/43: Schuster/Bordis; 44: T. Miček; 44/45: Ernst; 45: Dossenbach; 46/47: Image Bank/Beebe; 48: L. Miček; 48/49: T. Miček; 50/51: Siegel; 52/53: T. Miček; 53: T. Miček; 54 l.: L. Miček; 54/55: R. Maier; 56 l.: L. Miček; 56/57: T. Miček; 58/59: Reinhard; 60/61: V-Dia-Verlag; 62 l.: Explorer/Miche; 62 r.: Archiv für Kunst u. Geschichte, Berlin; 63 l.: Explorer/Marok; 63 r. o.: Schuster/Hoffmann-Burchardi; 63 r. u.: Explorer/Nardin; 64/65: Grafik: Zellweger; 66/67: Bavaria/Lauter; 68 l.: DPA; 68 r.: DPA; 69 l.: DPA; 69 r.: DPA; 70 l.: Hahne; 70/71: L. Miček; 71 r.: Schuster/Hirschmann; 72: Isenbügel/Barmettler; 73 l.: Brandl; 73 r.: Brandl; 74/75: Brandl; 76/77: Isenbügel/Barmettler; 78: Dossenbach; 78/79: Image Bank/Turner; 79: Dossenbach; 80/81: Image Bank/Turner, 82 o.: Dossenbach; 82 u.: Dossenbach; 83 o.: v. Hoorick; 83 u.: Dossenbach; 84/85: v. Hoorick; 86/87: Image Bank/Utoff; 88 l.: Reinhard; 88/89: Reinhard; 90/91: Reinhard; 92/93: Weiland; 93: Reinhard; 94 l.: Reinhard; 95 o.: Reinhard; 95 u.: Reinhard; 96/97: Reinhard; 98: Reinhard; 99 o: Reinhard; 99 u.: Reinhard; 100/101: Reinhard; 102/103: R. Maier; 103 o.: T. Miček; 103 u.: T. Miček; 104/105: Rapho/Zefa/Silvester; 106: T. Miček; 106/107: R. Maier; 108 o.: Rapho/Silvester; 108 u.: L. Miček; 109: T. Miček; 110/111: T. Miček; 112/113: L. Miček; 114/115: L. Miček; 116/117: T. Miček; 118: T. Miček; 118/119: L. Miček; 120/121: L. Miček; 122: Rapho/Silvester; 123 o.: Rapho/Silvester; 123 u.: Rapho/Silvester; 123 r.: R. Maier; 124/125: L. Miček; 126/127: L. Miček; 128/129: Rapho/Silvester; 130 o.: Dorian Williams; 130/131: Explorer; 132/133: Explorer/Loirat; 134 o.:

Schuster/Dimpe; 134 u.: Fenn/Ege; 135 o.: Bavaria; 135 u.: Explorer/Fiore; 136: Explorer/Dupont; 137 o.: Schuster/Fiore; 137 u.: Schuster/Fiore; 138/139: Archiv f. Kunst u. Geschichte, Berlin; 140/141 o.: Explorer/Valentin; 140/141 u.: Explorer/Valentin; 141: Archiv f. Kunst u. Geschichte, Berlin; 142/143: Archiv f. Kunst u. Geschichte, Berlin; 144/145: Cramm; 146: Löbl-Schreyer; 147 o.: Löbl-Schreyer; 147 u.: Löbl-Schreyer; 148: Bavaria/Galliphot/J. Challet; 148/149: Bavaria/Galliphot/J. Challet; 150 o.: Naturalis Archiv; 150 u.: Baravia/Bernhaut; 150/151: DPA/Bernhaut; 152/153: Archiv f. Kunst u. Geschichte, Berlin; 154: Archiv f. Kunst u. Geschichte, Berlin; 154/155: Archiv f. Kunst u. Geschichte, Berlin; 156/157: Roebild/Müller; 158/159: Weiland; 160/161: DPA; 162/163: Weiland; 164 o.: United Pictorial Press; 164/165: Reinhard; 166/167: Dossenbach; 168 l.: T. Miček; 168 o.r.: T. Miček; 168 u.r.: T. Miček; 168/169: T. Miček; 170 l.: Dossenbach; 170 r.: Dossenbach; 171 l.: Dossenbach; 171 r.: Dossenbach; 172/173: Grafik: Zellweger; 174/175: Sperber; 176: Sperber; 177: Sperber; 178/179: Bild Nr. 1) Dossenbach; 2) Dossenbach; 3) Dossenbach; 4) Dossenbach; 5) Wagner; 6) Dossenbach; 7) Dossenbach; 8) Dossenbach; 9) Dossenbach; 10) Dossenbach; 11) Dossenbach; 12) Dossenbach; 13) Dossenbach; 14) Dossenbach; 15) Dossenbach; 16) Dossenbach; 17) Dossenbach; 18) Dossenbach; 19) Dossenbach; 20) Dossenbach; 180/181: St. Georg; 182/183: V-Dia-Verlag; 184: Keystone; 184/185: Keystone; 186/187: T. Miček; 187 l. o.: T. Miček; 187 l. m.: T. Miček; 187 l. u.: T. Miček; 187 r.: T. Miček; 188/189: T. Miček; 192: T. Miček; 193 l.: Roebild/Müller; 193 r.: T. Miček; 194/195: alle Aufnahmen (5): T. Miček; 196/197: Zefa/Massner; 198/199: T. Micek; 200/201: T. Miček; 202/203: T. Miček; 203: T. Miček; 204/205: Bild Nr. 1) Anthony/Maier; 2) Barmettler/Isenbügel; 3) Dossenbach; 4) Dossenbach; 5) Dossenbach; 6) Dossenbach; 7) Dossenbach; 8) Rasa; 9) Dossenbach; 10) Dossenbach; 11) Dossenbach; 12) Wothe; 13) Dossenbach; 14) Dossenbach; 15) Roebild/Lorenz; 16) Dossenbach; 17) Dossenbach; 18) Dossenbach;

19) Bildarchiv Schuster; 20) Dossenbach; 206/207: T. Miček; 208/209: Reinhard; 210 l. o.: Dossenbach; 210 r. o.: T. Miček; 210 u.: Anthony Verlag; 211: T. Miček; 212/213: Prenzel; 213 l.: Fenn; 213 r.: Weiland; 214/215: Shostal Ass., New York; 216/217: Mauritius; 218/219: Rapho/Michaud; 220: Ploeger; 220/221: Rapho/Zefa/Michaud; 221: Explorer/Desjardin; 222/223: Ploeger; 224 o.: Ploeger; 224/225 o.: Explorer/Desjardin; 224/225 u.: Rapho/Zefa/Michaud; 225: Plöger; 226/227: Rapho/Michaud; 228: Zimmermann; 229: Anthony/Deuther; 230 l.: Lauert; 230 r.: Weiland; 231: Anthony/Deuther; 232/233: Dossenbach; 234/235: Zimmermann; 236: Weiland; 236/237: Kaufmann; 238/239: Anthony/Curth; 240/241: Peyer; 241 l.o.: Lauert; 241 m. o.: Lauert; 241 r. o.: Lauert; 241 u.: Zefa/Bordis; 242/243: Zefa/Weiland; 244: DPA; 245 o.: Weiland; 245 u.: Keystone; 246/247: Ernst; 248 l.: DPA; 248/249: Peyer; 250/251: Schuster/Hörnlein; 252 l.: Peyer; 252 o.: Zimmermann; 252 u.: Zimmermann; 253 o.: Zimmermann; 253 u.: Zimmermann; 254/255: Presse-Foto Baumann; 256 l.: Zimmermann; 256 r.: Dossenbach; 257 l.: Dossenbach; 257 r.: Sperber; 258 l.: Weiland; 258 r. o.: Zimmermann; 258 r. u.: Zimmermann; 259 o.: Zimmermann; 259 u.: Weiland; 260/261: Ernst; 262 l.: Peyer; 262 r.: Peyer; 263: Bavaria/Hubrich; 264/265: Zimmermann; 265: Zimmermann; 266/267: Presse-Foto Baumann; 268 l.: Peyer; 268 r.: Peyer; 269: Zimmermann; 270: Presse-Foto Mühlberger; 271 l.: Presse-Foto Mühlberger; 271 r.: Presse-Foto Mühlberger; 272 o. l.: Ernst; 272 o. r.: Ernst; 272 m. l.: Ernst; 272 m. r.: Ernst; 272 u. l.: Zimmermann; 272 u. r.: Ernst; 273: Peyer; 274/275:Zimmermann; 276/277: Presse-Foto Baumann; 278/279: Presse-Foto Baumann; 280 o.: Presse-Foto Baumann; 280 u.: Mauritius/Escher; 281 o.: Explorer/Blond; 281 u.: Klimke; 282: Roebild/Scuitto; 283 o.: Zimmermann; 283 u.: Dossenbach; 284/285: Presse-Foto Mühlberger; 286/287: Zimmermann; 287 o.: Presse-Foto Baumann; 287 u.: Presse-Foto Baumann; 288/289: Ernst; 290/291: alle Fotos (6) Zimmermann; 292/293: Zimmermann; 294 o.: Zimmermann; 294/295: Zimmermann; 296/297: Zimmer-

mann; 298 l. o.: Zimmermann; 298 r. o.: Zimmermann; 298 u.: Zimmermann; 299: Zimmermann; 300/301: Zimmermann; 302/303: Zimmermann; 304/305: Zimmermann; 305 o.: Anthony/Deuter; 305 u.: Art Reference/Zimmermann; 306/307: Zimmermann; 308/309: AllSport/Greenland; 310/311: alle Fotos (5) Zimmermann; 312 o.: Zimmermann; 312 u.: Zimmermann; 313 l.: Zimmermann; 313 o.: Zimmermann; 313 r.: Zimmermann; 314/315: Grafik: Mattei; 316/317: Dossenbach; 318/319: Zimmermann; 320/321: Zimmermann; 321: Peyer; 322/323: Zimmermann; 323 l. o.: Zimmermann; 323 l. u.: Peyer; 323 r. u.: Zimmermann; 324/325: Zimmermann; 326/327: Zimmermann; 328 l. o.: Zimmermann; 328 r. o.: Zimmermann; 328 r. u.: Peyer; 329: Zimmermann; 330: Zimmermann; 330/331: Schuster/Bordis; 332/333: Zimmermann; 334 o.: Zimmermann; 334 u.: Zimmermann; 335: Zimmermann; 336/337: Weiland; 338/339: DPA; 340 o.: George A. Smallsreed/U.S. Trotting ASSN; 340/341: Zimmermann; 342/343: Zimmermann; 344 o.: Zimmermann; 344 u.: Zimmermann; 344/345: Werek; 346 o.: Zimmermann; 346 u.: Zimmermann; 347 l.: Zimmermann; 347 r. o.: Dossenbach; 347 u.: Zimmermann; 348/349: Zimmermann; 350/351: Dossenbach; 352/353: Zimmermann; 353: Zimmermann; 354: Dossenbach; 354/355: Zimmermann; 356/357: Weiland; 358: Zimmermann; 358/359: Zimmermann; 360/361: DPA; 362/363: Okapia; 364/365: Isenbügel/Barmettler; 366: Bavaria/Chmelik; 366/367 o.: Sperber; 366/367 u.: Dossenbach; 367 o.: Kaup; 367 u.: Weiland; 368/369: Kaup; 370: Schuster/Dietrich; 371 o.: Kaup; 371 u.: Reinhard; 372/373: Anthony/Krohn; 374: Weiland; 375: Zimmermann; 376/377: Isenbügel/Barmettler; 378/379: Weiland; 379 o.: Image Bank/Stokes; 379 u.: Zefa/Schmied; 380/381: Image Bank/Steedman; 382: Schieren; 383: Naturalis Archiv